Byōbu: JAPANESE SCREENS FROM NEW YORK COLLECTIONS

Byōbu

JAPANESE SCREENS FROM NEW YORK COLLECTIONS

Miyeko Murase

THE ASIA SOCIETY, INC.

Distributed by New York Graphic Society Ltd.

Byōbu: JAPANESE SCREENS FROM NEW YORK COLLECTIONS is the catalogue of an exhibition shown in the Asia House Gallery in the winter of 1971 as an activity of The Asia Society, to further greater understanding between the United States and the peoples of Asia.

An Asia House Gallery Publication

Printed in the United States of America

Library of Congress Catalogue Card Number 74-134207

SBN: 0-87848-035-8

Contents

Acknowledgments 7

Lenders 8

Introduction 9

Chronology 17

Plates and Catalogue 18

Bibliography 134

Acknowledgments

OUR EXHIBITION OF BYŌBU—Japanese Screens from New York Collections—seems to have been born under the protection of favorable planets. A benevolent star first shone upon it from the Mary Livingston Griggs and Mary Griggs Burke Foundation, whose trustees have generously made it feasible to borrow these rare and beautiful panels of painted paper. To this illumination of our path was soon added the connoisseurship of Professor Miyeko Murase, a distinguished scholar in the field of Japanese painting, who kindly agreed to select the screens and to write the text of their catalogue. But it would still have been only a pleasant prospect had not the collectors and institutions of art that possess these treasures been so well disposed—each and every owner responding favorably to our requests for loans.

The leading private lenders on this occasion are Mr. and Mrs. Jackson Burke, who have supplied us with seven screens from their notable collection of Japanese art. As always, New York's great Metropolitan Museum of Art has been generously responsive, lending us for this display seven of their precious screens. Among them is a particularly notable work, "The Tales of the Hōgen and Heiji Insurrections" (No. 20), which Mr. Fong Chow kindly allowed us to include following its first presentation in "Masterpieces of Fifty Centuries" in their own galleries.

Nothing under the stars, it is believed, is beyond the reach of their controls. So it will have been thanks to these same planets that Dr. Roger Gerry, the owner of No. 9, "The Four Accomplishments," a screen attributed to Kanō Motonobu, acceded to our request to lend—and to borrow from others on our behalf the choice group of country potteries that are here used to complement the screens. We have also endeavored to thank him, and them, through an insert in this catalogue that identifies the owner and the provenance of each jar.

Because of the limited size of Asia House Gallery, we have been encouraged to offer this exhibition of Byōbu in two parts. The first part will be shown from January 14th through February 14th, the second part opening on February 16th and running through March 14th, the last day of the show. This close succession of the two sections makes it possible to display twice as many screens as we could otherwise have managed, giving visitors a double chance to become acquainted with some of the finest Japanese screens from New York and vicinity. We have ranged, as will be seen, as far as Princeton, N.J., to include the beautiful "Hozu Rapids" by Maruyama Ōkyo.

Gordon Bailey Washburn
Director
Asia House Gallery

Lenders to the Exhibition

The Brooklyn Museum, New York City
Mr. and Mrs. Jackson Burke, New York City
Mr. Martin Carr, New York City
Mr. Robert Ellsworth, New York City
Dr. and Mrs. Roger Gerry, Roslyn, N. Y.
Mr. and Mrs. Mathias Komor, New York City
Mrs. Marion Joseph Lebworth, New York City
The Metropolitan Museum of Art, New York City
Mr. and Mrs. Earl Morse, New York City
Mr. and Mrs. John G. Powers, New York City
The Art Museum, Princeton University, New Jersey
Mr. and Mrs. John D. Rockefeller 3rd, New York City

Introduction

THE WORDS "Japanese screen paintings" immediately evoke the sensuous beauty of brilliantly colored flowers and birds, painted against a glistening background of gold paper. Such screens can be found in great numbers at temples and palaces in Kyoto, and they are a joy to those who visit this ancient city. Screens have been collected by Europeans and Americans not only as objects of art, but also as striking decorations which enrich interiors with their bold designs and jewel-like colors. In traditional Japanese houses, however, beautifully painted screens were used not merely as decorations, but primarily as partitions or enclosures within interiors. Most of the screens so lavishly decorated with colorful paintings were produced from the late sixteenth through the nineteenth centuries. But screens were produced in Japan almost from the beginning of her history, and they developed as an indispensable element of Japanese architecture and an integral part of Japanese life.

Fig. 1. Ban Dainagon Ekotoba (Scroll Painting of The Story of the Courtier Ban Dainagon). Fujiwara Period, late twelfth century; color on paper. Tadahiro Sakai, Toyko.

Painted Japanese screens may be divided into three types. The first, *tsuitate*, which originated in China, is a small, one-panel, wooden screen, supported by low, wooden legs (Fig. 1). In *tsuitate*, the painting is sometimes executed directly on a wooden surface, but more often it is first done on paper, which is then pasted on the wood. The second type, the sliding screen, developed in the Early Heian period (794–897) as a partitioning device and a semipermanent fixture in Japanese buildings. Some sliding screens are made solely of wood, with decorations painted directly on the surface. These wooden doors are usually installed in corridors to separate one section of the building from the other. Another, more important type of sliding screen is *fusuma*, which is made of several layers of paper stretched over light, wooden lattice doors. The final layer of paper (or sometimes cloth) is usually decorated with a picture or with abstract designs. *Fusuma* were known in ancient Japanese as *sōji* or *shōji*. The latter name is used in modern Japanese for a screen which has white, semitranslucent paper stretched over latticed wooden frames. This is a much later type, which originated sometime in the Kamakura period (1185–1333). But the term was originally used to refer to sliding screens which had painted decorations. Within the buildings, tracks are made in the transverse beams above, and parallel tracks in the floor below, so that the sliding screens can be opened and closed according to need. The flexible spaciousness achieved by these sliding screen walls has influenced many modern architects in the West.

The third type, the folding screen (*byōbu*), is the only one represented in the present exhibition. *Byōbu* had a remote origin in China, as they were quite commonly used in the Han Dynasty (206 B.C.–221 A.D.). But the Japanese realized the full aesthetic potentialities of the *byōbu*, making it a strikingly effective form of interior decoration. The word "*byōbu*" implies an "enclosure" or a "protection against" (*byō*) the wind (*bu*), and the *byōbu* was used as a temporary divider of interior space (Fig. 2) or as an enclosure outdoors (Fig. 3). The *byōbu* is particularly convenient, since it can be folded into a portable size and transported easily or stored away when not in use.

As sliding screens are a semipermanent part of architecture, their size is regulated by the size of the buildings where they are installed. This is not quite true of a *byōbu*, which is made in a variety of sizes to suit a specific function or the taste of the period. Most commonly, a *byōbu* is made as a pair of six-fold screens, each measuring approximately five feet high and twelve feet wide. Smaller ones, measuring less than three feet in height, became popular especially after the seventeenth century. There are also eight-panel screens (No. 14) and two-panel screens (No. 7).

In 686 A.D. a *byōbu* was sent as a gift from the Silla Kingdom in Korea to the Japanese court,[1] and *byōbu* were also imported from China. The *Tōdaiji Kemmotsu Chō*,[2] an inventory of treasures donated to Tōdaiji by the Imperial family, includes one hundred folding screens. This suggests that by the mid-eighth century, *byōbu* were in common use at the court and in the homes of noblemen. Among the treasures housed in the Shōsōin at Nara is a set of screens representing beautiful women under trees. These mid-eighth-century screens are not only the oldest extant folding screens of Japan, but are also rare examples, as they were constructed in an ancient manner. In this method, each panel was surrounded by a wooden or silken border separating one panel from the next, and the panels were then tied together at top and bottom by leather or silken cords.

Fig. 3. Taima Mandara Engi Emaki (Scroll Painting of The Legend of the Taima Mandala). Kamakura Period, thirteenth century; color on paper. Kōmyōji, Kanagawa.

Fig. 2. Genji Monogatari Emaki (Scroll Painting of The Tale of Genji). Fujiwara Period, mid-twelfth century; color on paper. Tokugawa Museum, Nagoya.

A six-panel screen of the late eleventh century, known as the "Senzui Byōbu," formerly in Tōji, Kyoto, but now in the Kyoto National Museum, is an example of a *byōbu* made in this ancient manner but at a much later date (Fig. 4). This screen is also old-fashioned in its subject matter, which is derived from Chinese secular literature. The Chinese gentleman depicted in this screen is supposedly Po-chü-i, a great poet-scholar of the T'ang Dynasty (618–906), who has retired to his favorite mountain retreat and there receives his friends. Long before this screen was painted, Chinese themes as a subject of painting had gone out of fashion, only to be revived at a later date.

During the period from the late ninth to the late eleventh centuries there was a gradual development of a truly Japanese style with greater emphasis on native themes in the arts, and screen paintings must have undergone a similar process of evolution. Unfortunately, except for the "Senzui Byōbu," no screen painting from this critical period exists today; our study of screens illustrating native themes depends primarily on information given in contemporary literature.[3] According to literary references, at this time the screens at the Imperial palace and in the homes of noblemen most often illustrated famous views of Japan and the festivals and ceremonies in celebration of the seasons of the year. Such paintings depicting native subjects are called Yamato-e (Japanese painting) as distinguished from Kara-e (Chinese-inspired painting).

Yamato-e are mentioned in literature usually in relation to screens, suggesting that screens were the most common format for Yamato-e at this time. The evolution of Yamato-e is, therefore, closely involved with screens, yet because of the lack of early examples, *emaki-mono* (narrative scroll paintings) are often mistakenly regarded as the sole representatives of Yamato-e, while in reality they are but one form of this genre. *Emaki-mono*, however, are indispensable in a study of Yamato-e screens, as they often depict the interiors of houses, where painted screens are shown in miniature scale. These representations, in fact, are the only visual material available for a study of Yamato-e screens of the Fujiwara and Kamakura periods. They help us to reconstruct the general features of these screens which depicted, in bright colors, members of the aristocracy and commoners enjoying outings to famous scenic spots around Kyoto, or participating in seasonal ceremonies and celebrations. Activities associated with the coming of a new season constitute a vital aspect of Japanese life, both ancient and modern, and together with the depiction of seasonal changes in the landscape they remain important subjects of Japanese screen paintings throughout history.

Fig. 4. Senzui Byōbu. Fujiwara Period, late eleventh century; color on silk. Kyoto National Museum.

Colorful Yamato-e screens were gradually replaced by Chinese-inspired screens—monochrome ink paintings. The concept and technique of ink painting were introduced from China in the Kamakura period as a by-product of Zen Buddhism, whose concepts were best expressed in this medium. These subdued, monochrome paintings, the antithesis of Yamato-e, were slowly accepted as interior decoration, at first in Zen temples and only later in the homes of noblemen. No screen with ink painting made in the Kamakura period exists today, but again the screens represented in interior scenes in *emaki-mono* are invaluable sources of information.

With the official encouragement of the Ashikaga shoguns, ink painting almost replaced traditional polychrome painting in the Muromachi period (1336–1573). It came to be regarded as the ultimate form of painting and the only medium worthy of an important artist. Most of the extant early ink paintings of this period, however, are small hanging scrolls, as they had a better chance of survival than the screens, which often perished in buildings ravaged by wars, fires, and earthquakes. This historical accident sometimes gives the false impression that ink painters in the earlier years of this period preferred hanging scrolls to screens. However, most artists of the Muromachi period used both formats. A famous painting by Josetsu, "Catching a Catfish with a Gourd," was made originally for a *tsuitate*, and was only later remounted as a hanging scroll. Another well-known painter in ink, Shūbun, also created screens, and several extant *byōbu* are attributed to him. A sizable number of ink-painted screens of the late Muromachi period have survived and two of these, by Sōami (No. 8) and Motonobu (No. 9), are included in the present exhibition.

The ideal decoration for rooms in the living quarters of a cultivated Zen abbot was a set of screens with ink paintings that evoked the quiet, meditative mood inspired by their idealized landscapes, or renditions of famous Chinese scenery such as the confluence of the Hsiao and Hsiang rivers in south China. Even the human figures represented on these screens were derived from Chinese history and legends. In short, these ink paintings, totally Chinese in inspiration, created a contemplative, scholarly atmosphere appropriate for the occupant of rooms in the Zen temple.

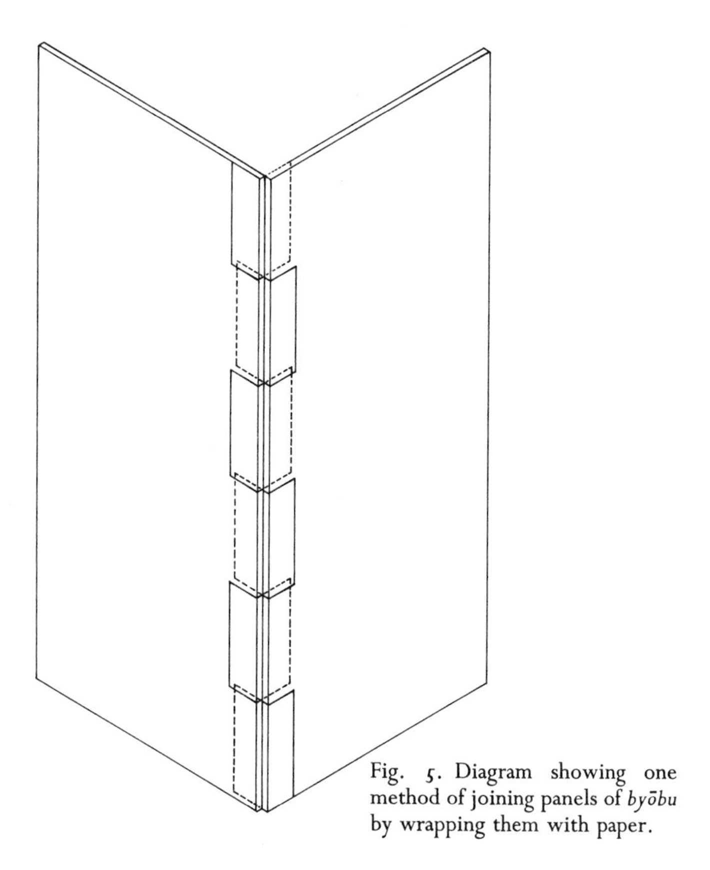

Fig. 5. Diagram showing one method of joining panels of *byōbu* by wrapping them with paper.

There are visual and literary sources which serve to reconstruct the plan of decoration for sliding screens in the Zen temple. The subjects of these sliding screens, usually landscape, figures, and flower-and-bird combinations, were selected by patrons to suit the specific position and installation within the building. Patrons often prescribed a particular Chinese style to be employed in painting these screens, for instance, in the "Mu-ch'i manner" or in the "Hsia Kuei manner." The sliding screens used as partitions between rooms are often installed on two or more sides of the room. A painted decoration which covered many panels on more than one side of a room was conceived as one long, continuous composition. Close-up views of landscape details were usually placed in the corners, while a panoramic, bird's-eye view was adopted for the intervening areas. This compositional device creates an illusion of greater space and perspective in the interior setting.

These general principles were also observed, to a certain extent, in painting freestanding, folding screens. There, greater freedom prevailed in selecting the subject, style, and composition, because the spaces to be decorated were not restricted to the walls of a room. Also, an innovation of purely technical nature, which had been introduced in the mid-fourteenth century, contributed to the development of better and more unified compositions for folding screens. The broad borders surrounding each panel of the ancient *byōbu* were replaced by a new type of frame whose edges are visible only at the top and bottom of each panel and at the outer sides of the panels at each end. This change was made possible by the invention of a new method of joining the panels. The leather or silken cords which had linked the panels of the ancient screens were abandoned. In the new method, still in use today, strips of paper are wrapped horizontally from the front of one panel to the back of the next, forming hinges. The adjacent strips are applied in the reverse direction, as shown in the diagram (Fig. 5). This process is repeated at least three times to strengthen the hinges. The separations between panels are thus minimized and all sections of the screen are united visually within one large frame. Each panel may then be treated as a part of a large, uninterrupted composition.

The landscape screens attributed to Shūbun share one important compositional feature which dominates almost all screen paintings of the later periods. A large picture surface created by combining a pair of screens is divided into three sections: one section at the extreme right, another in the center occupying the adjoining halves of each screen, and the third at the extreme left. The forms in the extreme right and left panels are depicted as if viewed from close range, while the central area is seen as if from a distance or from a bird's-eye point of view. In keeping with the Far Eastern custom of writing, we "read" these screens from right to left. We first examine the close-up view of nature at the right, then move to a panoramic view of a body of water, and finally arrive at another close view. This scheme is clearly expressed in the screens of "The Four Accomplishments" attributed to Motonobu (No. 9). Rocks, trees, waterfalls, and human figures in the extreme right and left panels are depicted in large, clear forms defined by strong brush strokes. The central area is occupied by a panoramic view of the distant water, marshland, and low-lying mountains, represented in soft, light ink washes.

The three-part composition is a convenient framework for the depiction of seasonal changes in landscape paintings. As we "read" screen paintings from right to left we experience the seasonal progression from spring to winter: spring at the extreme right; summer and autumn in the central area; the snowy winter landscape at the extreme left. Most painters of the Muromachi and later periods observed this basic principle of composition in painting landscapes and other subjects on folding screens.

With few exceptions, Muromachi screen paintings were executed solely in ink. The calm, contemplative atmosphere created by a subtle play of ink greatly appeals to us today. To some contemporary critics of Shūbun, however, monochrome screen paintings were not quite satisfactory as interior decorations. One of his critics, Prince Gosukō-in, a man of keen aesthetic insights, once described a monochrome screen painting by Shūbun as "still unsatisfactory and not quite successful."[4] This brief comment seems to suggest that Shūbun's ink paintings lacked a desirable, essentially decorative quality.

Sesshū (1420–1506), the greatest landscape painter of this period, introduced several features which helped to restore this decorative quality to sombre monochrome screens. By using stronger and more emphatic brush strokes Sesshū defined forms clearly, and by constructing his pictorial elements in a rational, architectonic manner, he achieved structural stability in his compositions. At the hands of Sesshū, ink paintings on screens lost some of their subtle beauty, but they regained a pleasing quality which was needed for interior decoration. This quality is most pronounced in a group of screens usually attributed to Sesshū which depict flowers, birds, and trees of the four seasons. In these screens, the new techniques of ink painting are employed effectively, and also strong colors are reintroduced and successfully fused with ink. This new trend started by Sesshū was later perfected by two early masters of the Kanō school, Masanobu (ca. 1434–ca. 1530) and Motonobu (1476–1559), who established the canons of screen painting for centuries thereafter. The spiritual and ennobled world of pure monochrome landscape by Sōami (d. 1525) stands in marked contrast to Motonobu's harsher yet more decorative expression of nature; in the screens of these two artists, whose styles and principles differed widely although they were almost contemporaries, an important change occurs in room decoration of the early sixteenth century.

The Momoyama period (1573–1614) marks a golden age in screen painting when many works not only of high quality but also of widely varied subject-matter and style were created. It was a "golden" age in the literal sense of the word, as real gold was applied liberally on many screens. Paper-thin gold sheets cut in large squares were applied to entire surfaces; small gold flakes were freely sprinkled for decoration; and gold pigment was used along with ink and colors. The use of gold on screens was not, however, the invention of Momoyama artists, for its history dates to the fourteenth century. As early as the beginning of the fifteenth century it was recorded that golden screens were exported in large numbers to Korea and China, where they were treasured, along with swords and folding fans, as Japanese specialties.[5]

Literary sources of the mid-fifteenth century refer to a sharp increase in the local demand for gold screens.[6] They were used at funeral rites in Buddhist temples, and in the homes of cultivated men as convenient backdrops on which to display hanging scrolls of painting and calligraphy. The literary records of the period frequently refer to golden screens; to the increased demand for them, to their scarcity (which forced some people to borrow them from friends for special occasions), to damages caused to them, and to their having been pawned for small sums of money.

The introduction of firearms by the Portuguese, ca. 1543, had revolutionized warfare and architecture. As defense against the powerful new weapons, castles with strong fortifications were built in many parts of the country. Their interiors were lavishly decorated with screens painted in colors and gold, symbolizing the might and wealth of the emerging war lords. One of the earliest to be erected in this period was Azuchi Castle, built for Oda Nobunaga (1534–1582), who first united the war-torn country after the fall of the Ashikaga shoguns. Nobunaga commissioned young Kanō Eitoku (1543–1590), grandson of Motonobu, to decorate the interior of this seven-story castle, which was completed in 1576 only to be razed in war six years later. However, there is a detailed description of Azuchi Castle and its decoration in the biography of Nobunaga, the *Shinchō-kō Ki*.[7] It was considered most sumptuous and fashionable, and became the model for other castles and palaces. Every room was decorated with screens; their subjects were largely flowers, trees, birds, and animals, as well as human figures derived from Chinese literature and history. Most of these screens were painted in dazzling colors against a shining gold ground; only one landscape, the "Eight Views of Hsiao and Hsiang," seems to have been painted in ink. The list of flora and fauna painted here by Eitoku and his assistants recalls the repertory commonly found on extant Momoyama screens. There were bamboo, paulownias, pines, plums; hawks, geese, pheasants, phoenixes; and also dragons, horses, and tigers. Many of these were symbolic of the power and vigor of the emerging class of military men.

Nobunaga's successors and other war lords, men of arms but little sophistication, followed suit by building their own castle-palaces. These buildings boldly proclaimed the new power and wealth, and their interiors, shining in opulence and dazzling extravagance, reflected the spirit of the age. There are enough sliding screens preserved in their original locations to permit a reconstruction of the general scheme of room decoration in castles and palaces. Ink paintings, mainly of Chinese figures and landscapes, were often chosen as decoration in private living quarters. Paintings representing Japanese narrative or genre subjects were preferred for the smaller, less formal reception rooms. Large audience halls, designed for grand, formal receptions, were usually decorated with paintings of flowers, birds, and animals in brilliant colors and heroic designs.

The author of the *Shinchō-kō Ki* also comments on Eitoku's technique and touches upon his style. He remarks, half critically and half admiringly, that Eitoku was so busy that he "did not have time to paint small details." This is an apt observation, one which applies to many extant screens attributed to him. The forms filling these screens are large and clearly defined by broad brush strokes (Fig. 6). The compositions are simple, and the colors bright and vivid. Their effect is immediate and direct; they were made to impress the crowds that gathered in large rooms. During the day, the golden screens with their ostentatious but masculine designs shone from the darkest corners of audience halls, while at night they reflected the flickering light of hundreds of candles. As room decorations they were also an ideal solution to problems of interior lighting.

Members of the Kanō school, as well as most other painters of this period regardless of their school or training, painted screens for castles, palaces, and Buddhist temples. They moved with great ease from one style to another, at times using the ink-painting technique, at others dazzling colors and abstract

Fig. 6. Screen Paintings by Kanō Eitoku, in the Jukō-in, at Daitokuji, Kyoto. Ca. 1566 (in the style of the early Momoyama Period); ink, color, and gold on paper.

designs. With the same ease they switched from one subject to another—historical, narrative, decorative, landscape, or genre. A monopoly of subject matter simply did not exist. For example, Eitoku, who is best remembered for paintings of lions, hawks, pines, and cypresses of heroic grandeur, also painted a genre picture of scenes inside and outside Kyoto, and his screens illustrating the *Tale of Genji* are examples of painting derived from classical Japanese literature. All artists of the Momoyama period possessed diversified talents and worked in different modes, a fact which makes the study of their works exciting and difficult.

For the most part, screen painters of the Edo period (1615–1867) continued the Momoyama tradition. Recognized artists, and their works, are so numerous as to make it impossible to review them here. However, a few schools deserve special mention. Painters of all schools practised the style invented by the Kanō painters, which combined the brilliant colors and native subject matter of Yamato-e with the Chinese ink technique (No. 14). This was also true of the Tosa school, the champion and guardian of the Yamato-e tradition. It is often difficult to distinguish Yamato-e from other types of painting, as a line separating the Tosa and Kanō schools is not always clear. In the mid-nineteenth century a small group of artists lamented the decline of Yamato-e and made special efforts to revive it. This group, known as the Fukko Yamato-e Ha (school of Yamato-e Revivalists), includes Tanaka Totsugen (d. 1859), Ukita Ikkei (1795–1859), and Okada Tamechika (1823–1864). However their paintings, being politically inspired and supporting the movement to restore the sovereignty of the Imperial family, did not recapture the vitality of the Yamato-e tradition.

A genuine revitalization of the Yamato-e tradition was brought about in the paintings of Sōtatsu and his colleagues and followers. This group includes the great designers whose names are familiar to connoisseurs of Japanese art: Kōetsu (1558–1637), Kōrin (1658–1716), Roshū (1699–1757), and Hōitsu (1761–1828). Their screens are well represented in number and quality in the present exhibition (Nos. 1–7). Few of these men had experienced the classic relationship of pupil and mentor, as their lifetimes were separated. In spite of this fact, their paintings share one important feature: a stunning beauty of abstract pattern, often inspired by classical literary themes. They were motivated by a desire to express the truly native spirit in a new idiom, and their works mark a peak in Japanese painting. To most of these painters, the ancient Japanese traditions of subject matter and technique often served as the starting point for their personal development.

The Nanga painters and the Realist group of artists worked from different premises. Nanga (Southern School painting), also known in Japan as Bunjinga (Literati painting), derives its concept and models from Chinese Literati paintings of the Ming and Ch'ing dynasties. The Chinese Literati artists—gentlemen painters of the landed gentry who worked purely for their own aesthetic satisfaction—were held in highest esteem. In contrast, the Nanga painters of Japan were not members of the landed gentry but professional artists. They welcomed the opportunity to decorate screens, and some of the early Nanga artists such as Ike Taiga (1723–1776) and Yosa Buson (1716–1783) painted many screens, as for example Buson's "Landscape in 'Mi' Style" (No. 11). One of the characteristics of true Nanga painting is the use of ink as the primary medium, sometimes combined with light washes of color. Still, on occasion, Nanga artists deviated from this principle, and Taiga painted screens with bright colors on gold, a far cry from the ideals of Southern School painting in China. Yet, in brush technique and subject matter, most Nanga painters remained loyal to the Chinese models.

The Realist painters Maruyama Ōkyo (1733–1795) and Matsumura Goshun (1752–1811) advocated direct observation and objective portrayal of nature, as is beautifully illustrated in their screens in this exhibition (Nos. 12, 13). Although they adhered to the Chinese ink and brush technique, their subjects were drawn from familiar Japanese scenery and people. Moreover, inspired by their contact with Western concepts and techniques, they perceived nature in new ways.

Painters who never signed their screens and who therefore remain nameless in history, form a class apart, and they have come to be known as Machi-eshi (town-painters). Many of these anonymous artists seem to have been trained in the Tosa or Kanō schools. They were employed by shops selling screens that were mass-produced and primarily intended to appeal to the less discriminating plebeian patrons who preferred genre subjects. Merchants of the Edo period had attained the wealth, security, influence, and leisure that had previously been denied them. For this class of patron the Machi-eshi produced a new type of picture. The pictorial themes which had been but small elements in large screens, such as those depicting scenes inside and outside Kyoto (No. 22), gradually became independent topics in genre paintings. Among the favorite themes are the cherry blossom- and maple-viewing picnics, the Gion Festival, the Kamo horse race, the archery contest at Sanjūsangen-dō, dog-chase games, the Kabuki and Noh theatres, and above all, scenes of pleasure quarters and the beautiful women of these districts. These subjects were by tradition depicted on folding screens, but the dimensions of the screens decreased markedly to conform to the smaller residences of the new patrons. Genre scenes which were easy to understand had an immediate appeal to the less-educated, less-sophisticated audience of the age.

Japanese screen paintings of the Momoyama and Edo periods offer a comprehensive panorama of the varied schools and subjects. They are a continuing source of aesthetic pleasure as well as valuable material for the study of Japanese life and the aspirations of her people.

1. *Nihongi; Chronicles of Japan from the Earliest Times to A.D. 697*, trans. W. G. Aston (London, 1956), p. 376.
2. *Nara Ibun* [Documents from the Nara Period], Vol. II, ed. Rizō Takeuchi (Tokyo, 1962), pp. 433–459.
3. Terukazu Akiyama, *Secular Painting in Early Mediaeval Japan* [Heian Jidai Sezoku-ga no Kenkyū] (Tokyo, 1964); Alexander C. Soper, "The Rise of Yamato-e," *Art Bulletin* 24 (1942), pp. 351–379; Kenji Toda, "Japanese Screen Paintings of the Ninth and Tenth Centuries," *Ars Orientalis* 3 (1959), pp. 153–166.
4. *Kammon Gyoki* [Diary of Gosukō-in], ed. Zoku Gunsho Ruijū Kanseikai (Tokyo, 1944), p. 533, in the entry for April 9 of the tenth year of the Eikyō era (1438).
5. *Yijo Sillok* [History of the Yi Dynasty], ed. Gakushū-in Tōyō Bunka Kenkyū-jo, vol. IX (Tokyo, 1953–), p. 350, in the entry for November of the twenty-fifth year of Emperor Se-jong's reign (1443); *Kaitei Shi-seki Shūran* [Collection of Historical Documents, Revised], ed. Keizō Kondō (Tokyo, 1900–1916), vol. XXI, *Zenrin Kokuhō Ki* [Records of the Muromachi Government's Diplomatic Relations with China and Korea], vol. II, p. 35, in the entry for the ninth year of the Ōei era (1403).
6. Eiji Akazawa, "On the Gilt Folding-Screens in the Fifteenth Century" [Jū-go Seiki ni okeru Kin Byōbu ni tsuite], *The Kokka*, no. 849 (December 1962), pp. 567–579; Tsuneo Takeda, "On Konpeki Shōheki Mural" [Kompeki Shōheki-ga ni tsuite], *Ars Buddhica* (December 1965), pp. 105–122.
7. *Kaitei Shi-seki Shūran*, vol. XIX.

Chronology

Heian Period 794–1185

Early Heian 794–897

Fujiwara 898–1185

Kamakura Period 1185–1333

Muromachi 1336–1573

Momoyama 1573–1614

Edo 1615–1867

1. The Tale of Genji

Edo period, seventeenth century; School of Sōtatsu
Eight-fold screen; color on gilded paper; H. 36¾ in., W. 133½ in.
Signature: "Sōtatsu Hokkyō"; Seal: "Taisei-ken"
Published: Yūzō Yamane, *Sōtatsu* (Tokyo, 1962), pls. 42, 43
Lent by Mr. and Mrs. Jackson Burke

OPPOSITE:
The Tale of Genji (detail).

GENJI MONOGATARI, the *Tale of Genji*, is perhaps the best-known literary work of Japan. This great romance of the amorous adventures of Prince Genji was written at the beginning of the eleventh century by Murasaki Shikibu, a lady-in-waiting at the court. The novel seems to have become a favorite subject for paintings shortly after its completion. The oldest extant scroll painting (*emaki-mono*) inspired by this novel dates from the middle of the twelfth century, but only a fraction of what once must have been a large set of scroll paintings remains today. The *Tale* has remained the most frequently illustrated Japanese novel, and it enjoyed a revival of interest in the Momoyama and Edo periods, perhaps as a reaction against the overwhelming influence of Chinese art in the Muromachi period. Many artists of various schools, including those of the traditional Tosa school and the Chinese-inspired Kanō painters, illustrated this story. The painters of the Sōtatsu-Kōrin school also used this subject.

In this version a wide band of gold, almost one-third of the entire height of the screen, crosses the foreground. On this golden sand, pines with twisted trunks and branches grow. Finger-like cloud patterns in gold are used in the traditional manner to divide the remaining picture surface into a series of cells and compartments inhabited by charming, youthful noblemen and long-haired ladies, direct descendants of twelfth-century types. Their eyes are mere slits and their noses, simple hooks. This technique, known as *hikime-kagihana* (dashes for the eyes and hooked line for the nose), was used in the Genji scrolls of the twelfth century. The curious convention of eliminating the roofs from some houses, known as *fukinuke-yatai* (houses with blown-off roofs), was also used in the Genji scrolls. It allows the viewer to see the interior without obstruction.

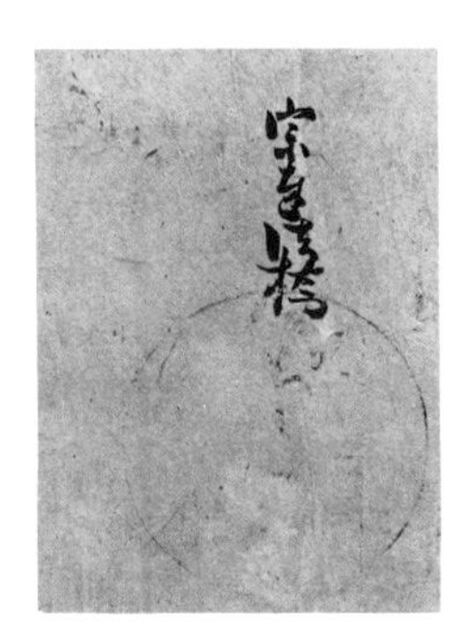

Nine episodes are illustrated on this eight-panel screen. With the exception of the eighth panel (counting from right to left), each panel has one scene selected from each of seven chapters, namely chapters nineteen through twenty-five. The two scenes in the last panel represent episodes chosen from chapter twenty-six. Since the screen illustrates a small but continuous section of a novel consisting of fifty-four chapters, probably there were more screens to accompany this one; together they would form a complete cycle of illustration. In fact, two or three more screens of this type are known, although most of the pictures are now separated from the screens and have been remounted as hanging scrolls.[1] Perhaps these screens were made originally as a large set, each screen illustrating an average of six to eight chapters, with one or two scenes from each.

The scene on the first panel of this screen illustrates an episode from chapter nineteen (Wreath of Cloud). The consort of the ex-emperor, Fujitsubo, whom Genji loved dearly, died at the age of thirty-seven. Overcome with grief, Genji retired into his chapel, and at sundown he "found a flaming sun about to sink beneath the horizon. Against this vivid glow, the trees upon the hill stood out with marvelous clearness . . . but across the hill there presently drifted a thin filament of cloud, draping the summit with a band of grey."[2] The scene on the second panel represents an episode from chapter twenty (*Asagao* [Morning Glory]). On a cold winter night the full moon shone "out of a cloudless sky upon the glittering, fresh-fallen snow" in the garden.[3] Genji and his second wife, Murasaki, look out into the garden and watch children make an enormous snowball near a frozen pond. The third panel illustrates an episode from chapter twenty-one (The Maiden). Yūgiri, Genji's young son, tries to talk to his childhood love, Kumoi, who is about to be sent away from him to live at her father's palace. Yūgiri "stood upon the threshold looking so disconsolate that his old nurse could not bear it."[4] The scene in the fourth panel shows an episode from chapter twenty-two (Tamakatsura). Tō-no-chūjō's daughter, Tamakatsura, who had been reared in secrecy in Kyūshū makes her long journey back to the capital in search of her father.[5] The fifth panel shows a scene from chapter twenty-three (The First Song of the Year). Murasaki celebrates the third day of the New Year in her apartment, when Genji makes an unexpected entry.[6] The sixth panel describes a happy festival from chapter twenty-four (The Butterflies). A colorful pageant is staged on Genji's estate. Little boys, some dressed as birds, some as butterflies, come from Murasaki's garden in a Chinese boat. They bring cherry blossoms and other flowers as offerings to the Buddha.[7] The seventh panel illustrates an episode from chapter twenty-five (The Glowworm). Genji tries to persuade his ward, Tamakatsura, to talk to his brother, Prince

Sochi, who wishes to court her; the Prince stands in the corridor.[8] Two scenes in the eighth panel illustrate Genji's frustrating attempts to seduce Tamakatsura; these are described in chapter twenty-six (A Bed of Carnations). In the upper scene, Genji talks to her; in the lower, after demonstrating a few notes on the *koto* (thirteen-stringed, zither-like musical instrument), which is partly hidden behind a *byōbu*, he admires her beauty.[9]

The seal, reading "Taisei-ken," and signature, "Sōtatsu Hokkyō," are placed at the lower right-hand corner of this screen. The seal "Taisei-ken" (7.7 cm. in diameter) is also impressed on the screens of the "Royal Visit to Ōhara" (No. 2). It is also found on many scrolls and screens which have come to be associated with Sōtatsu. This seal is often used in combination with the signature "Hokkyō Sōtatsu" or "Sōtatsu Hokkyō." A word must be said here about this reversal of the order of the name and the title. Hokkyō is a priestly title which was originally conferred by the Imperial court on scholarly priests, but Jōchō, the sculptor of the Amida Buddha at Byōdō-in at Uji, became the first artist to receive this, in 1022. After that time many artists were awarded the same honor or even higher ones. Sōtatsu seems to have been granted the title shortly after 1621. The correct usage of the title in a signature is to place it before the personal name, thus the correct order would be "Hokkyō Sōtatsu." By reversing it, "Sōtatsu Hokkyō" becomes informal, and it might imply the "studio of Sōtatsu who was a Hokkyō," and not "Sōtatsu with the title of Hokkyō."

Yūzō Yamane, in his book *Sōtatsu*,[10] discussed the problem of Sōtatsu's seals and signatures. He discovered that the combination of the "Taisei-ken" seal and the "Sōtatsu Hokkyō" signature is most often found on ink paintings and less frequently on screens. The problem of Sōtatsu's seals and the question of the attribution of his paintings are extremely complex.

Although Sōtatsu is perhaps one of the greatest and most popular painters of Japan, few facts about his life are known and there is uncertainty as to the dates of his birth and death, and his family name. In spite of the work of several scholars, only a few facts have emerged. According to these findings, Sōtatsu was the leader, perhaps the owner, of a prosperous fan-making studio known as Tawara-ya. The shop was particularly cherished by the citizens of Kyoto for its beautifully colored pictures of the *Tale of Genji*. It is interesting that there are extant many fan paintings associated with Sōtatsu and his studio.

According to a genealogical chart in the possession of the Kataoka family, Sōtatsu married a cousin of Kōetsu (1558–1637). Kōetsu was a connoisseur, calligrapher, potter, and designer who gave artistic guidance to many artists and artisans. He seems to have written poems on many scrolls which were painted by Sōtatsu. Perhaps it was through Kōetsu's influence and friendship with court nobles that Sōtatsu was commissioned to repair, in 1602, some of the Lotus Sutra scrolls, known as the "Heike Nōkyō," at the famous Itsukushima Shrine. In 1621, Sōtatsu painted the screens at Yōgen-in in Kyoto. This temple was rebuilt at the order of the wife of Tokugawa Hidetada, the second Tokugawa shogun. It is quite possible that Sōtatsu was granted the title of Hokkyō as a reward for this work. In 1630 he made two copies of scrolls illustrating the life of priest Saigyō that were originally painted in 1500 by Kaida Unume. Sōtatsu seems to have died shortly after he made these *emaki-mono*. In 1642, a painter named Sōsetsu, who also used the Tawara-ya name of the fan shop, signed his painting with the title of Hokkyō, indicating thereby that he was the successor to Sōtatsu.

Since Sōtatsu was the leader of a studio, it is quite likely that some paintings attributed to him were actually executed by members of his studio. The Genji screen in the present exhibition seems to be a studio work, with traces of the great master's styles. Sōtatsu's marks are particularly evident in the landscape passages of this screen and in the use of the *tarashikomi* technique by which darker colors are applied on wet, lighter pigments, creating a blurred effect. However, the figures are much more delicate than those found in other paintings generally accepted as actual works of Sōtatsu.

1. Yamane, *op. cit.*, p. 210.
2. Lady Murasaki, *The Tale of Genji*, trans. Arthur Waley (New York, 1960), p. 374.
3. *Ibid.*, p. 395.
4. *Ibid.*, p. 419.
5. *Ibid.*, pp. 434–466.
6. *Ibid.*, p. 467.
7. *Ibid.*, pp. 482, 483.
8. *Ibid.*, p. 494.
9. *Ibid.*, pp. 507–523.
10. *Op. cit.*, pp. 228–237.

OPPOSITE:
The Tale of Genji (detail).

2. Royal Visit to Ōhara

Edo Period, seventeenth century; School of Sōtatsu
Pair of six-fold screens; color on paper; H. 65¾ in., W. 148½ in., each screen
Seal: "Taisei-ken" on both screens
Published: Shūjirō Shimada, ed., *Zaigai Hihō* [Japanese Paintings in Western Collections], vol. II (Tokyo, 1969), pl. 53
Lent by The Metropolitan Museum of Art; Fletcher Fund, 1955

TWO COURTIERS ON HORSEBACK, followed by their attendants, enter a narrow mountain path from the right side of the right screen. There are workmen and travelers around a farmhouse. On the left screen, more noblemen and their retainers are assembled in the courtyard of a country house.

The painting illustrates the last chapter of the *Tale of the Heike* (*Heike Monogatari*), a historical novel of the mid-thirteenth century. The *Heike Monogatari* describes the late-twelfth-century struggle for power between the Heike (the Taira clan) and the Genji (the Minamoto family). It also recounts the splendors and the eventual fall of the Taira, thus forming a sequel to the *Tales of the Hōgen and Heiji Insurrections*. The last chapter of the *Heike Monogatari* relates the tragic life of Kenreimon-in, daughter of the head of the Taira clan, Kiyomori, and mother of the infant emperor Antoku, who drowned in the sea of Dan-no-ura along with the Heike family. After the fall of the Heike, Kenreimon-in entered retirement at the Jakkō-in nunnery in Ōhara, northeast of Kyoto. In May of 1186, the ex-emperor Goshirakawa, who had already abdicated and taken Buddhist vows, decided to pay a visit to Kenreimon-in. In this quiet mountain hide-out, the summer season was just beginning:

> . . . . . . the young grass grew thick and the green shoots of the willow were tangled . . . . . the purple of the flowering wisteria mingled with the green of the pine; the late blooming cherry among the young leaves was even more wonderful than the early blossoms . . . . . From the clouds of kerria roses . . . . . came the call of the cuckoo, a note of welcome in honor of His Majesty's visit.[1]

This passage in the *Tale* is recreated faithfully on these screens: a bright, sunny atmosphere of early summer with myriad blossoms sets a stage for the royal visit to Ōhara. The vanguard of the royal group has already reached the nunnery, the humble country house portrayed in the extreme left panels of the left screen, and the ex-emperor, dressed in priestly robes, can be seen standing in front of it. Goshirakawa has called to Kenreimon-in but there has been no response, and on his face is a momentary expression of doubt and hesitation. He is then told that the ex-empress and her attendant are out taking a walk, gathering flowers in the hills. A steep mountain path rises behind the nunnery, where two women dressed in the gray-black habits of nuns may be seen. Kenreimon-in holds a sprig of azalea in her hands.

A feeling of the warm, quiet day in early summer is created by the lightly brushed gold dust in the sky and by the warm brown colors of trees and houses. The tragedy that has overtaken the once powerful Kenreimon-in and Goshirakawa is softened by the bright, sunny atmosphere and the beautiful flowers in bloom.

The red, round seal reading "Taisei-ken" is found in the extreme lower corner of each screen. This seal is identical with those found on many paintings associated with Sōtatsu and his studio. The same seal is also impressed on the screen that portrays the *Tale of Genji*, included in this exhibition (No. 1). There is a strong possibility that this seal was used not only by Sōtatsu himself but by members of his workshop as well. Therefore, the appearance of this seal alone does not guarantee Sōtatsu's authorship of these screens. It is undeniable, however, that there are strong traces of Sōtatsu's influence, especially in the use of the *tarashikomi* technique. Sōtatsu's influence is also apparent in the shapes of houses, trees, and rocks. The portrayal of human figures likewise reveals that the artist was familiar with the types of figures used by Sōtatsu. A curious feature of the painting is that the artist has combined several compositions used by Sōtatsu and his associates, creating something of a pastiche. For example, the courtiers on horseback and their retainers, a herd boy with his animal, and an ox tied to a pine tree, may be traced directly to the compositions painted on fans, screens, and scrolls which were produced by Sōtatsu and his assistants.[2]

1. Donald Keene, *An Anthology of Japanese Literature* (New York, 1955), p. 189.

2. Yamane, *Sōtatsu*.

Royal Visit to Ōhara (detail).

3. Irises and Bridge

Edo period, eighteenth century; by Ogata Kōrin (1658–1716)
Pair of six-fold screens; color on gilded paper; H. 70½ in., W. 146¼ in., each screen
Signature: "Hokkyō Kōrin" on the right screen, "Seisei Kōrin" on the left screen; Seals: "Masatoki" on both screens

Published: *Zaigai Hihō* II, pl. 59. Alan Priest, "Kōrin and the Iris Screens," *The Metropolitan Museum of Art Bulletin* 13 (March 1955), pp. 209–212
Lent by The Metropolitan Museum of Art; purchase, Louisa E. McBurney Gift Fund, 1953

A BENDING, angular footbridge extends from one panel to the next and from one screen to the other, crossing our field of vision boldly in a strong, diagonal sweep. On both sides of the bridge, in clustered groups, are borders of irises, arranged in a rhythmic orchestration of sharp blades and full blossoms. Brilliant green for the blades, violet-blue for the flowers, and gray-blue for the under petals—these vibrant colors are set boldly against a shining gold ground. The striking composition, of utmost simplicity, and the luxuriant beauty of sensuous colors make these screens unforgettable masterpieces of Japanese art.

The painting is also a prime example of Kōrin's decorative designs, many of which were derived from classical literature. It is stripped of all verbosity, to a degree that makes one forget that this is actually a rendition of an episode in the *Tale of Ise*.[1] In fact, it can be enjoyed just as a beautiful design in colors, nothing more. The *Tale of Ise*, a mid-tenth-century travel diary, consists of poems interspersed with connecting narrative vignettes or prose settings. It is generally attributed to Ariwara Narihira (824–880), one of the great romantic poets of Japan, but the identity of its true author still remains a mystery. A portion of the ninth chapter seems to reflect the imagery of the bridge, marshes, and irises in these screens:

> Once a certain man decided that it was useless for him to remain in the capital. With one or two old friends, he set out toward the east in search of a province in which to settle. Since none of the party knew the way, they blundered ahead as best they could, until in time they arrived at a place called Yatsuhashi in Mikawa Province. (It was a spot where the waters of a river branched into eight channels, each with a bridge, and thus it had come to be called yatsuhashi—"Eight Bridges.") Dismounting to sit under a tree near this marshy area, they ate a meal of parched rice. Someone glanced at the clumps of irises that were blooming luxuriantly in the swamp. "Compose a poem on the subject, 'A Traveler's Sentiments,' beginning each line with a syllable from the word 'iris' [kakitsubata]," he said. The man recited,
>
> I have a beloved wife,
> Familiar as the skirt
> Of a well-worn robe,
> And so this distant journeying
> Fills my heart with grief.
>
> They all wept onto their dried rice until it swelled with the moisture.[2]

Kōrin painted the subject of irises in a pond a number of times, with or without the bridge, and in different media. There are screens like this one in the Nezu Museum, Tokyo,[3] while the Tokyo National Museum has a lacquer box and a hanging scroll[4]; there is also a small round fan which depicts the same subject.[5] The hanging scroll in the Tokyo National Museum illustrates the poem most faithfully, since it includes the figures of Narihira and his friends viewing the iris flowers. As none of these works is dated, it is difficult to reconstruct the stages in Kōrin's development of this pictorial motif. However, we may hazard the guess that Kōrin proceeded from a more literary description, with figures, to the abstract design with flowers alone as in the Nezu screens. If our conjecture is correct, versions showing only irises and the bridge, as seen in the Metropolitan screens, the lacquer box, and the round fan, may belong to the same group. This group of works may have been made just before Kōrin evolved the composition, as in the Nezu screens, in which he stripped all the narrative elements and reduced the design to the stark purity of flowers alone. It is interesting that in the early nineteenth century Sakai Hōitsu reproduced the Metropolitan screens in his publication, *Kōrin Hyaku Zu* (One Hundred Selections from Kōrin). Hōitsu's own copy of these screens also exists today.

The life of Ogata Kōrin is full of dramatic events, an alternation of successes and disappointments. His life is well-documented and can be reconstructed almost year by year. This is due largely to the great number of papers and letters kept by Kōrin and ultimately given to his son.[6] His son was adopted by the Konish family, and descendants of this family have taken good care of these documents until recently, when some were placed in a private collection in Tokyo, the rest in the Osaka

Irises and Bridge (detail).

Municipal Museum. Many are dated, the earliest being from the time when Kōrin was fifteen. Some papers deal with personal activities of Kōrin and his family, some letters concern Kōrin's scandalous and well-publicized extra-marital affairs, and there are even some pawnshop tickets. In this quantity of material there are also seals used by Kōrin and a large number of sketches and preliminary drawings that he made.

Kōrin was born to a prosperous cloth merchant of Kyoto who was known by the name of the family business, Karigane-ya, which sold goods to the shoguns and the Imperial family. The artist had the carefree childhood of a well-protected son, learning all the necessary accomplishments required of a man of genteel upbringing. Kōrin may also have been acquainted with the paintings of Sōtatsu and his mentor, Kōetsu. Kōrin's great-grandmother was an older sister of Kōetsu, and according to one source, Sōtatsu was married to Kōetsu's cousin. A family relationship may therefore have existed among the three great artists who established the canons of decorative painting in the Edo period.

Kōrin's life as a wealthy gentleman was suddenly altered by financial reverses a few years after his father's death in 1687. He was bankrupt, and he began to visit pawn shops frequently from about 1694; on one occasion, he even pawned Kōetsu's ink box and a water jar. Kenzan (1663–1743), Kōrin's younger brother, was an accomplished potter, who opened a kiln in 1699 to support himself. Kōrin, having neither occupation nor money, was invited to help Kenzan; a happy collaboration between a great potter and a great painter materialized. Kōrin's daring design and fluid style of painting soon found a wide market, and shortly afterwards he began working as an independent artist. Meanwhile, in 1701, Kōrin received the rank of Hokkyō from the court, a title which is found in the signatures of many of his paintings.

Kōrin greatly admired the art of Sōtatsu and made copies of some of his paintings; among these copies are the screens of Wind God and Thunder God in the Tokyo National Museum,[7] and the screens representing Matsushima in the Museum of Fine Arts, Boston.[8] Kōrin's interest in paintings derived from the classical literature of Japan is also traced to Sōtatsu and Kōetsu. The *Tale of Ise*, one of these classics, was often illustrated by Sōtatsu, and Kōrin continued in this tradition. Kōrin, however, did not merely follow the Kōetsu-Sōtatsu tradition. By systematically dismissing superfluous elements, he achieved a truly individual art of rare decorative beauty.

1. Helen Craig McCullough, *Ise Monogatari; lyrical episodes from tenth-century Japan* (Stanford, 1968), pp. 74, 75.
2. *Ibid.*
3. Elise Grilli, *The Art of The Japanese Screen* (Tokyo, 1970), pp. 109–120, pls. 49–54.
4. Ichimatsu Tanaka, *Kōrin* (Tokyo, 1965), pls. 28, 62.
5. *Ibid.*, pl. 41.
6. Yūzō Yamane, *The Life and Work of Kōrin*, vol. I, *The Konishi Collection* [Konishi-ke Kyūzō Kōrin Kankei Shiryō to sono Kenkyū] (Tokyo, 1962).
7. Tanaka, *op. cit.*, fig. 108.
8. *Ibid.*, pl. 23.

Irises and Bridge (detail).

4. The Pass through Mt. Utsu

Edo period, eighteenth century; by Fukae Roshū (1699–1757)
Two-fold screen; color on gilded paper; H. 28½ in., W. 74 in.
Seal: "Roshū"
Published: Sherman E. Lee, *Japanese Decorative Style* (Cleveland, 1961), no. 84. Hiroshi Mizuo, "Tsuta-no-hosomichi Zu Byōbu" [A Folding Screen Picture of Tsuta-no-hosomichi], *The Kokka*, no. 767 (February 1956), pp. 34–39
Lent by Mrs. Marion Joseph Lebworth

A PASSAGE in the ninth chapter of the *Tale of Ise*, immediately following the episode represented in the "Irises and Bridge" screens in the Metropolitan Museum of Art (No. 3), describes an event in which Narihira, the hero of the story, meets a mendicant priest at a vine-covered, narrow mountain pass, Utsu-no-yama. The poem and the prose read:

> On they journeyed to the province of Suruga. At Mount Utsu the road they were to follow was dark, narrow, and overgrown with ivy vines and maples. As they contemplated it with dismal forebodings, a wandering ascetic appeared and asked, "What are you doing on a road like this?" The man, recognizing him as someone he had once known by sight, gave him a message for a lady in the capital:
>
> Beside Mount Utsu
> In Suruga
> I can see you
> Neither waking
> Nor, alas, even in my dreams.[1]

In this narrow, two-paneled screen, large, round hills and rocks provide the setting for the episode. Ink is splashed on brown and green hills in *tarashikomi*, a favorite technique of the Sōtatsu-Kōrin school. Small pine trees, with short, twisted trunks, hug the hillside. Against the gold background, red ivies and the blue dress of the court nobleman give luminosity to the otherwise muted color. The hills, set wide apart to suit the format of the screen, are slightly in conflict with the description in the text of a dark and narrow path. Another inconsistency is that, according to the story, the nobleman, presumably Narihira himself, meets the priest coming toward him down the path. The painting, however, depicts the monk, carrying a large sutra box on his back, climbing up the pass, away from the courtier.

These discrepancies in Roshū's version are easy to understand when we compare this painting with two earlier renditions of the same subject made by Sōtatsu[2] and Kōrin.[3] Roshū relied heavily on the paintings by these great masters of the past. None of these artists considered it necessary to follow the text closely. Roshū made two more versions of the same subject, one of which is in the Cleveland Museum of Art,[4] and the other in the Umezawa Kinen-kan Museum in Tokyo.[5] These, both six-fold screens, are much larger than the Lebworth screen; they are also more complex in composition and closer in design to the Sōtatsu and Kōrin paintings. Perhaps the Lebworth screen is the artist's last and most individualized variation on this subject. By eliminating nonessential elements from the picture, Roshū achieved an effect of loneliness overtaking the solitary traveler at an isolated mountain pass.

Fukae Roshū was long regarded as a mysterious artist, and some facts about his life have come to light only recently. He was the eldest son of Fukae Shōzaemon, a colleague of Nakamura Kuranosuke who was a flamboyant patron of Kōrin. Shōzaemon was an official at the government mint (*Ginza*); he, as well as Kuranosuke and two other officials, was expelled from office and sent into exile in 1714 as a result of a scandal involving bribery and fraud. It was perhaps through his father's connection with Kuranosuke that Roshū came to know and admire Kōrin's paintings. However, it is doubtful that Roshū received Kōrin's personal instruction, since he was only sixteen years of age when Kōrin died.

1. McCullough, *Ise Monogatari*, p. 75.
2. Yamane, *Sōtatsu*, p. 174.
3. *Zaigai Hihō* II (Text), p. 86.
4. *Ibid.*, II, pl. 67; Lee, *op. cit.*, no. 83.
5. *Zaigai Hihō* II (Text), p. 89; Hiroshi Mizuo, "Tsuta-no-hosomichi Zu Byōbu" [A Folding Screen Picture of the Chapter of Tsuta-no-hosomichi in the Ise Monogatari Tale], *The Kokka*, no. 819 (June 1960), pp. 222–225.

The Pass through Mt. Utsu (detail).

5. Trees and Flowers by a Stream

Edo period, eighteenth century; School of Sōtatsu-Kōrin
Pair of six-fold screens; color on paper; H. 48 in., W. 123 in., each screen
Published: D. J. R. Ushikubo, *Life of Kōyetsu* (Kyoto, 1926), pl. facing p. 24 (left screen). S. C. Bosch Reitz, "The Magnolia Screen by Kōyetsu," *The Metropolitan Museum of Art Bulletin* 11 (January 1916), pp. 10–12. Ernest Fenollosa, *Epochs of Chinese and Japanese Art*, vol. II (New York, 1912), p. 134
Lent by The Metropolitan Museum of Art; left screen, Rogers Fund, 1915; right screen, gift of Horace Havemeyer, 1949

A LARGE STREAM flows from one panel to the next and from one screen to the other. Slow, gentle waves suggest the depth and force of its current. Along the river's banks grow the trees and flowers of spring and autumn. On the right screen are a pine tree and the spring blossoms of pear, peach, azalea, and irises. On the left are magnolia, maple, and gingko trees, pampas grasses and asters. The spring flowers are all white, except for a little red azalea. On the other screen, the somber mood of autumn is brightened by the ginko and maple leaves ablaze in yellow and red. The bank of the river is covered with small silver flakes, now darkened with age. The muted color scheme and the gentle flow of the mountain stream create an effect of serene isolation in a silent forest.

There is neither signature nor seal on these screens, but Fenollosa praised them in his book as genuine works of Kōetsu,[1] and his opinion was repeated by some others.[2] However, modern scholars are generally skeptical that Kōetsu was a serious and successful painter, and these screens should be reexamined from a fresh point of view. The curious, geometric shapes of rocks in dark green, blue, and brown, seen at the extreme right of the right screen, is found frequently in paintings by artists who were influenced by Sōtatsu. On the other hand, the exaggerated, step-like bend of the magnolia tree on the left screen is a typical feature of trees found in paintings by the followers of Kōrin, such as Watanabe Shikō (1683–1755) and Tatebayashi Kagei (early eighteenth century). The screens shown here display less decorative distortion and abstraction than do many of the known works by Sōtatsu and Kōrin. But this is more than compensated by a marked degree of descriptive realism in detail, a trend which may be noted in many eighteenth-century followers of these two masters.

1. Fenollosa, *op. cit.*, p. 134.

2. Bosch Reitz, *op. cit.*, pp. 10–12; Ushikubo, *op. cit.*, p. 25.

Right screen

Trees and Flowers by a Stream. Left screen.

6. Persimmon Tree

Edo period, dated late autumn of 1816; by Sakai Hōitsu (1761–1828)
Two-fold screen; color on paper; H. 64 in., W. 65¼ in.
Signature: "Hōitsu Kishin"; Seal: "Monsen"
Published: National Museum of Tokyo, ed., *Illustrated Catalogue: The Exhibition of the Sōtatsu-Kōrin School* [Sōtatsu-Kōrin Ha Zuroku] (Tokyo, 1951), no. 110. "Kaki Zu Kai" [A Persimmon Tree], *The Kokka*, no. 526 (September 1934), pp. 245, 246
Lent by The Metropolitan Museum of Art; Rogers Fund, 1957

MOST OF THE WELL-KNOWN works by Hōitsu are in rich, brilliant colors applied over a gold or silver ground. This screen, showing a persimmon tree, is very different. A single tree grows from the lower left against an unpainted, natural-colored paper. Only a few leaves cling to the branches, and round, red, ripe fruits are heavy and ready to fall. Brown pampas grass and other wild grasses around the roots of the tree are the only other motifs in this painting. A simple color scheme of red, green, and touches of brown, with light washes of ink, together with a large void area, give a feeling of the clear, crisp air of late autumn, just before the arrival of cold winter.

The serenity and simplicity of this screen are indeed rare among Hōitsu's colorful paintings. A few realistic details on the tree and fruits reflect his earlier interest and training in the naturalistic style of Ōkyo.

Sakai Hōitsu was born in Edo, the second son of the Lord Sakai of Himeji. Early in life he showed a keen interest in painting and first studied with a Kanō master; he then experimented in the Chinese style and also with Ukiyo-e, the popular form of genre painting that depicted the "Floating World" (*Ukiyo*) of fugitive pleasures. He moved to Kyoto in 1797, when he adopted the priestly name of Monsen Kishin used in the seal and signature on this painting. In Kyoto, he also admired the realistic paintings of Ōkyo. His admiration of Kōrin seems to have developed rather late in his life, only after he had studied many other styles of painting. Since one of his ancestors was a patron of Kōrin, Hōitsu may have had the means to acquire paintings by this artist. In 1815, one year before he made this painting, Hōitsu celebrated the centennial of Kōrin's death by publishing *Kōrin Hyaku Zu* (One Hundred Selections from Kōrin) in which the paintings are reproduced in wood-block prints. These reproductions, of paintings which were considered by Hōitsu and his contemporaries to be genuine works of Kōrin, give valuable guides to connoisseurship of Kōrin's works.

7. Cypress Trees

Edo period, nineteenth century; by Ikeda Koson (1802–1867)
Two-fold screen; ink on paper; H. 59 1/16 in., W. 65 in.
Signature: "Koson Sanshin Renshin-kutsu ni oite utsusu";
Seals: "Saga Sammai-an Shu" and "Sanshin"
Lent by Mr. and Mrs. Mathias Komor

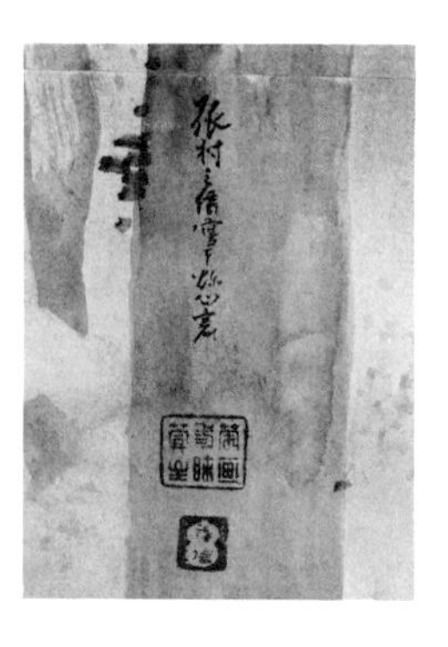

IKEDA KOSON and his colleague, Suzuki Kiichi (1796–1858), are regarded as the two best students of Hōitsu. Koson followed the style of his teacher and also echoed him by publishing a book on Kōrin, *Shinsen Kōrin Hyaku Zu* (A New Series of One Hundred Selections From Kōrin). Together with Hōitsu's book, it offers valuable information for a study of Kōrin's work.

In this exquisite painting, we see the work of an artist of extraordinary talent and sensitivity who moved away from the traditional style of the Sōtatsu-Kōrin school, which relies on brilliant colors and bold designs. The subject of the painting is the cypress, one of the favorite motifs used by many painters of that school. Koson's painting consists of the trees alone, as in Hasegawa Tōhaku's famous "Pine Grove." Like Tōhaku, Koson uses ink exclusively. He expresses the essence of the subject with economy of means, and achieves a decorative effect in a quiet and subtle manner. Ink tones vary from pitch black to pearl gray. The leaves have a uniformity of shape and size that might deceive us into thinking that Koson had prepared patterns with which to paint them, as Kōrin sometimes did. Tree trunks, large and small, are delineated by soft, vertical brush strokes, without outlines; the use of *tarashikomi* technique creates a blurred effect. A light wash of ink and the small ink dots on the ground convey a feeling of quiet, slightly damp woods, into which the soft rays of the sun stream intermittently.

8. Landscape of Four Seasons

Muromachi period; by Sōami (d. 1525)
Pair of six-fold screens; ink on paper; H. 68¼ in., W. 146 in., each screen
Signature: "Kangaku Shinsō hitsu" on both screens; Seal: "Shinsō" on both screens

Published: *Zagai Hihō* I (Text), pp. 122, 123. Alan Priest, "A Pair of Sōami Screens," *The Metropolitan Museum of Art Bulletin* 36 (December 1941), pp. 243–245
Lent by The Metropolitan Museum of Art; gift of John D. Rockefeller, Jr., 1941

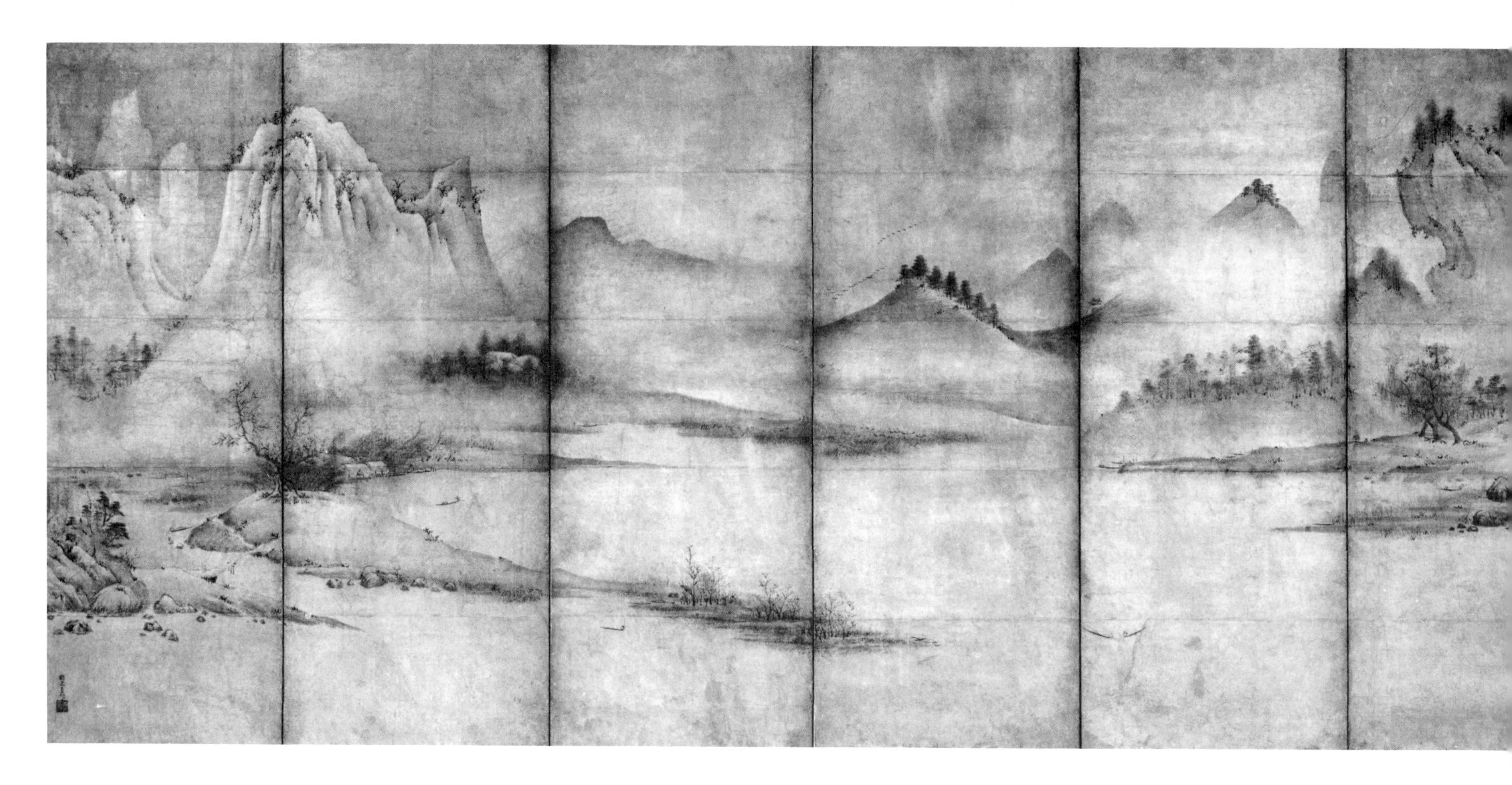

A BROAD BODY of water is surrounded by mountains and hills which close off the view in the distance like the backdrop of a stage. There are a few indications of human life, such as travelers over the bridge at the right, boats on the lake, and houses. But their existence is scarcely noted, and the landscape is strangely silent, with an air of mystery. The landscape is shown in four seasons: spring and summer, with its moist air and rich vegetation, on the right screen, autumn and winter on the left.

This work is a beautiful example of the technique of ink painting which combines soft, sfumato strokes with subtle washes. There are few harsh lines, except for a stark, skeletal tree in the winter scene. The soft style of painting was preferred in south China, especially for the Eight Views of Hsiao and Hsiang, which depicts the confluence of the Hsiao and Hsiang rivers. The style was considered peculiarly suggestive of the warm, humid, and misty climate of that region. Sōami is especially noted for the use of this technique, and his name is associated with many paintings of the Eight Views. The Metropolitan screens bear a strong similarity to the screens of the Eight Views in the Daisen-in of Daitokuji, Kyoto.[1] They also resemble a large hanging scroll in the Cleveland Museum of Art.[2]

Using only ink, Sōami creates a personal vision of an idealized, ennobled landscape in a faraway land, viewed in a contemplative mood. The painting is an expression of the essence of serene nature, an image which was held sacred by every Zen monk and ink painter of the Muromachi period.

Sōami, also known as Kangaku and Shinsō, belonged to the Ami group of the Jishū sect of Buddhism, founded by Priest Ippen in the thirteenth century as an expression of belief in Amida Buddha. Many members, identified by the word "Ami" in their names, were artisans and artists. Among these were painters of three generations whose names included the syllable "shin" and who are particularly famous: Shinnō (also known as Nōami, d. 1471), Shingei (Geiami, d. 1485 ?), and Shinsō (Sōami). It is still not clear whether these three were blood relations. At any rate, their position, *Karamono Bugyō*, was that of adviser and curator of art objects imported from China for the Ashikaga shoguns, and it seems to have been handed down from one "shin" to the next. This position enabled these Ami painters to become acquainted with Chinese paintings. Sōami, in 1511, finished the book, *Kundaikan Sayū Chōki*, a list of the Chinese painters represented in the shogunal collection at that time. The book, which was actually started by his predecessors, lists these painters in three categories of esteem. Sōami also edited another book, *Okazari Ki* (Notes on Decoration), which set a standard for interior decoration in the Shoin style of domestic architecture, including the arrangement of objects in recessed alcoves (*tokonoma*). In other words, Sōami was the taste-maker of the period, and some scholars maintain that it was he who popularized among Japanese painters the soft, misty style of ink painting.[3]

1. Hiroshi Kanazawa, "Shō-shō Hakkei Zu" [The Eight Scenic Spots in Hsiao Hsiang], *The Kokka*, no. 886 (January 1966), pp. 35–37.
2. *Zaigai Hihō* I, pl. 94.
3. Takaaki Matsushita, *Muromachi Suiboku Ga* [Ink Painting of the Muromachi Period] (Tokyo, 1960), Appendix I.

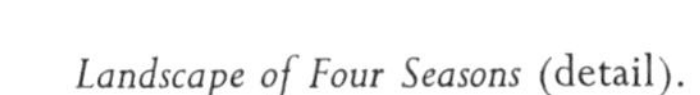

Landscape of Four Seasons (detail).

9. The Four Accomplishments

Muromachi period; attributed to Kanō Motonobu (1476–1559)
Pair of six-fold screens; ink and light color on paper; H. 67 in., W. 150 in., each screen
Seal: "Motonobu" on both screens
Published: "Kinki Shoga Zu" [The Four Accomplishments], *The Kokka*, no. 642 (May 1944), pp. 125, 126
Lent by Dr. and Mrs. Roger Gerry

SINCE ANCIENT TIMES in China, the arts of calligraphy, painting, music, and chess have been regarded as the four prerequisites of the Confucianists and gentlemen scholars. Paintings which represent men assembled for the enjoyment of these arts were often made in China, and were the indispensable possessions of the gentleman scholar. The concepts of the Four Accomplishments and paintings illustrating them were introduced to Japan in the Muromachi period, and many Japanese painters of various schools used this theme in their works.

The composition of these two screens is based on the tradition of painting a landscape viewed in four seasons (cf. Nos. 8, 10), which attained popularity in the fifteenth and sixteenth centuries. These two screens may be viewed as one continuous composition, with a stage for the picture established by the close-range views of landscape at right and left. The central area, where the two screens meet, recedes into the distance. At the right, large, crystalline rocks in the foreground and middle ground clearly define a three-dimensional space. An abundance of water in the stream suggests the spring season. On the stone bridge is a gentleman, accompanied by a youthful servant who carries his master's musical instrument, the *ch'in* (zither). Their attention is directed towards three friends who pay rapt attention to a game of chess. The pine tree stretches its branch over the shoreline; beyond it lie a low marshland and a vast expanse of water, with low-lying hills in the distance. Water birds fly away from the reed-covered marsh, creating the effect of an autumnal scene. In the screen at the left, two servants carrying bundles of books seem to have been startled by the sudden flight of birds, while their master is absorbed in deep thoughts. They are ascending the hill to the house of a friend, who stands at the verandah viewing the waterfall. Inside the room servants have unrolled a scroll, an ink painting. The time is winter, and traces of white snow may be seen on the thatched roof and rocks. The waterfall has the razor-edge sharpness of icy water. Throughout the painting crisp, hard outlines, and the strong contrast of dark and light ink define the form clearly. Colors are used sparingly, and the brush strokes are clear and obvious.

Motonobu's seal is impressed on each of the screens. However, Motonobu's seals are generally thought to be later additions; their existence alone cannot prove his authorship of these screens. The painting, however, reflects stylistic idiosyncrasies apparent in Motonobu's accepted works. Motonobu painted the subject of the Four Accomplishments many times. These screens in the Gerry collection are very similar, in style and composition, to another version of this subject by Motonobu at the Reiun-in of Myōshinji, Kyoto.[1]

Kanō Motonobu, son of Masanobu and grandfather of Eitoku, succeeded his father as official painter to the Ashikaga shoguns. At the same time he held a similar position at the Imperial court. Motonobu completely adapted the art of Chinese ink painting to suit a new function as decoration for interiors. His paintings were highly respected by contemporaries, and his screens were often sent to China by Japanese traders and envoys as gifts for Chinese officials. These found admirers even among some Chinese painters, one of whom addressed a letter to Motonobu saying that his paintings reminded him of works by the Sung dynasty artists, Ma Yüan and Chao Ch'ang.[2]

1. "Sansui Jimbutsu Zu" [Figures in Landscape]. *The Kokka*, no. 137 (October 1901), pp. 66, 67.
2. Shun Etō, "Motonobu ni kansuru Teitaku Sekitoku" [A Letter by Teitaku Addressed to Kanō Motonobu], *Yamato Bunka*, no. 35 (July 1961), pp. 72–74.

The Four Accomplishments (detail).

10. Landscape of Four Seasons

Momoyama period; by Unkoku Tōgan (1547–1618)
Pair of six-fold screens; ink and light color on paper; H. 69 in., W. 148 in., each screen
Seals: "Unkoku" and "Tōgan" on both screens
Lent by Mr. and Mrs. Jackson Burke

BY JUXTAPOSING DIAGONALS and verticals in these screens, Tōgan achieves a sense of structural stability and clarity. The seasons of spring and of summer, with its luxuriant growth, are shown in the right panels of the right screen (they continue into the right-hand corner of the next screen). In the far distance are gentle hills, seen in the autumn season. A few boats are on the water, and geese fly away. The autumn season continues into the next screen, where it is the dominant theme. Massive hills rise above the water in sheer verticality, but again the diagonal lines of smaller hills and pine trees counterbalance this forceful movement. Brown reeds bend on the shore. A lone man appears, moving over the bridge at the extreme left. Wintry hills may be seen in the distance to the right and left of the massif.

The flight of geese in the distance and the moon in the sky recall two scenes from the famous Eight Views of Hsiao and Hsiang. The subject itself implies seasonal changes, and it gained enormous popularity among Japanese landscape painters. In fact, the Japanese found this subject so congenial that they often borrowed scenes from the series and combined them with others of their own composition. Pale blue and orange-brown colors are used with utmost restraint, as is light gold dust sprinkled in the sky, water, and misty atmosphere.

This painting immediately recalls Sesshū's celebrated scroll of 1468, known as the "Long Scroll" because of its length of fifty-five feet. In Tōgan's screens, not only the sharp, obvious outlines, but also the shapes of rocks, houses, figures, and boats, and the clear, architectural structuring of landscape elements are derived from Sesshū's works.

Unkoku Tōgan, founder of the Unkoku school, assumed this family name after the name of Sesshū's studio, Unkoku-an in Yamaguchi at the southern tip of the island of Honshū. Lord Mōri, the ancestor of the present owner of Sesshū's "Long Scroll," gave Unkoku-an to Tōgan as a reward for having made a good copy of the scroll in 1593. Tōgan also claimed that he was the rightful heir to Sesshū's tradition, and he is said to have won a legal dispute about this designation against Hasegawa Tōhaku (1539–1610). Tōgan's descendants and followers, among them Unkoku Tōeki (1591–1644) and his older brother Unkoku Tōoku, remained active in southern Honshū and preserved Sesshū's tradition for many generations.

Landscape of Four Seasons (detail).

11. Landscape in "Mi" Style

Edo period, eighteenth century; by Yosa Buson (1716–1783)
One of a pair of six-fold screens; ink on paper; H. 57 1/8 in., W. 131 in.
Inscription: "Sanka-ken chū ni oite Bei Nangū o manabu"
Signature: "Sha Chōkō"; Seals: "Nōdō" and "Tōsei"
Published: Chū Yoshizawa, "Hō Ōmō Sansui Zu Byōbu [Landscape by Buson], *The Kokka*, no. 870 (September 1964), pp. 24–31. Tōru Mori, "Buson no Sansui Byōbu Issō" [Landscape Screens by Buson], *Kobijutsu*, no.4 (March 1964), pp. 105–110.
Lent by Mr. Robert Ellsworth

IN THIS SCREEN there is a gradual deepening of space in the distance. The foreground is clearly established by the flat shore with a cluster of trees. Empty houses, some inlets, and more trees are visible in the middle ground. Tall mountains rise suddenly and sharply from the flat land, looming high above vaporous clouds. The short, thick growth of shrubs on the mountains, the foliage of the trees, and the shoreline are all delineated in horizontal strokes—some short, some long; very few outlines are used in this painting. Subtle, but infinitely rich variations of ink tones help to create a light and airy atmosphere. There is only a hint of the presence of man. Two men walk over a bridge, and fishermen, barely visible, are seen at the extreme left. The vacant houses at right are strangely silent, and their blank walls and empty doorways seem to deny entry. The absence of human life in this painting is in keeping with truly Chinese tradition, and it marks a departure from the usual works of Buson. Buson, in his paintings and poetry, usually showed warm sympathy and a deep attachment to man and his world.

Buson, who enjoys great popularity in Japan and is known to Americans as one of the greatest poets of Japan, first became famous for haiku (a seventeen-syllable poem). A serious interest in painting developed rather late in his life, probably in his late thirties. Yet, together with Ike Taiga, (1723–1776), Buson is regarded as one of the two greatest Nanga (Southern School) painters of Japan. Nanga is also known in Japan as Bunjinga (painting by literary men), and its source is the theory of Chinese painting formulated by Ming and Ch'ing masters. Educated Japanese painters of the Edo period strove to imitate Chinese models. The Nanga painters aspired to grasp the principles of nature and of painting through the experience of travel and through a study of Chinese poetry and painting. Buson spent many years traveling all over Japan, spurred onward also by his involvement with haiku.

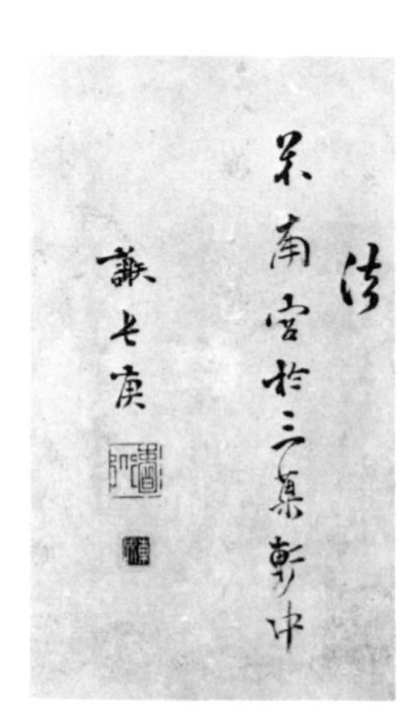

Landscape in "Mi" Style (detail).

As a true Nanga painter, Buson admired and copied works by the Chinese literati painters. He states in the inscription on this screen that he was at his Kyoto studio, Sanka-ken, when he painted it, and that in it he tried to imitate the style of Mi Fei. Mi Fei (1051–1107), who is idolized in China and Japan, is credited with inventing short, dot-like strokes, known as "Mi dots," which create an almost pointillistic effect. Buson used "Mi dots" almost exclusively in painting this screen. His admiration for Mi is also manifest in one of the seals he impressed on this painting. The word "nō" (*nang* in Chinese) of the seal "Nōdō" forms a part of one of the numerous poetic names used by Mi.

The former owner of this screen also possessed its companion piece, which is now in the collection of the Nobel Prize winner Yasunari Kawabata, in Kamakura.[1] The validity of pairing these two screens is sometimes doubted, although they are identical in size. The screen in the Kawabata collection was, according to Buson's inscription on it, painted in the style of Wang Meng (d. 1385), one of the four great masters of the Yüan dynasty. That screen also has the seal reading "Sanka Shujin" (master of the Sanka studio), and this fact establishes a direct connection with the screen in the Ellsworth collection, which was also painted at this studio. If, indeed, Buson made these screens as a pair, they form a startling contrast of styles. The "Wang Meng" screen is done in a dry, rough technique, while the "Mi Fei" screen is soft and misty. The Kawabata screen has an inscription which dates it to December 5, 1760, and this date may also apply to the Ellsworth screen.

1. Yoshizawa, *op. cit.*, pp. 25, 27; Mori, *op. cit.*, pp. 108–110.

12. The Hozu Rapids

Edo period, dated early summer of 1772; by Maruyama Ōkyo (1733–1795)
Six-fold screen; ink, light color, and gold on paper; H. 61½ in., W. 136¾ in.
Signature: "Ōkyo"; Seals: "Ōkyo no In" and "Chūsen"
Published: *Zaigai Hihō* II, pl. 75. Hiroshi Mizuo, "Hotsu-gawa Zu Fusuma-e" [The Hotsu River], *The Kokka*, no. 885 (December 1965), pp. 28–34
Lent by The Art Museum, Princeton University

THIS SCREEN, now in the form of a folding screen with six panels, was originally made as four sliding panels.[1] Traces of the original arrangement are still visible in the seam-like lines in the second and the fifth panels, and in the repairs made over the former sockets. This painting is believed to represent the Hozu Rapids, one of the best-known scenic places of Japan, located not far from Kyoto. But there is nothing in the treatment or description of the scene to make this identification a certainty.

Low but powerful waterfalls descend into a violent mountain stream whose turbulent current moves quickly across the foreground plane then gently fades from sight at the left. Before the stream becomes a leisurely, gentle flow, it passes through hard, jagged, crystalline rocks. The short, choppy, sharp strokes, which outline and give texture to these hard rocks and pine trees, echo the roar and misty spray of the current. Broader strokes and a lighter ink are used for the gentle, round hills at the left. Except for a light hue of gold dust sprinkled as mist above and below, and pale brown and blue which are hardly visible, the painting is done primarily in ink. Even the tone of ink is rather limited in range. Ōkyo was very fond of the rapid flow of water, for it offered him endless varieties of expression. He painted this theme many times, last in 1795 on a screen in the Nishimura collection.[2] The Princeton screen was painted in 1772, twenty-three years before that final version. It may lack the boldness and dramatic power of the Nishimura screen, but it has the quality of a real landscape with a true sense of depth and distance and minimal distortion of nature. Ōkyo revolted against the stiff, academic style of the Tosa and Kanō schools, preferring to depict nature as it is and as he saw it. This painting is a full reflection of his aesthetic principles.

Ōkyo was the founder of the Maruyama school of painting, which exerted influence on many artists of the nineteenth and twentieth centuries. He first studied the Kanō style with Ishida Yūtei (1721–1786), but soon became dissatisfied with its academic direction and with the traditional training method of copying old paintings and pattern books. As a young man he became acquainted with perspective and chiaroscuro in Dutch prints, and earned his living by making pictures used as sets for the peep-show (*megane-e*). Ōkyo then turned with seriousness to the Western technique of painting. He also practised the techniques of decorative Yamato-e and Chinese ink painting. He particularly admired the Yüan painter Ch'ien Hsüan (1235–1290), noted for his precise drawings of plants and insects. Out of respect for this Chinese painter he adopted the name Ōkyo, and a poetic name, Chūsen, both of which include Chinese characters used in Ch'ien Hsüan's own names. Ōkyo's greatest contribution is that he advocated the need for a direct observation of the natural world; practising his own theory, he made many sketches directly from nature. Ōkyo also spoke about his theories on painting and aesthetics, and one of his pupils, Oku Bummei (d. 1813), recorded and edited these opinions in a book, *Sensai Maruyama Sensei Den* (Life of the Master Maruyama).

1. Mizuo, *op. cit.*, pp. 30, 31.

2. *Zaigai Hihō* II (Text), p. 99; Mizuo, *op. cit.*, p. 33.

The Hozu Rapids (detail).

壬辰初夏寫
應擧

13. Woodcutters and Fishermen

Edo period; by Matsumura Goshun (1752–1811)
Pair of six-fold screens; ink and light color on paper; H. 67 ¼ in., W. 137 in., each screen
Signatures: "Goshun utsusu" on the right screen, "Goshun" on the left screen; Seals: "Goshun" and "Hakubō" on both screens
Published: *Zaigai Hihō* II, pl. 89
Lent by Mr. and Mrs. Jackson Burke

MATSUMURA GOSHUN STUDIED the art of haiku and of the Nanga school under Buson. During the time when he worked with Buson he used the name Gekkei. He adopted the name Goshun in 1781, and it is used in the seals and signatures on these screens. A few years after Buson's death, in 1783, Goshun met Ōkyo, who advised him to change his style from Nanga to the more naturalistic way of painting preferred by Ōkyo. Goshun never really abandoned his early Nanga training but he combined the poetic manner of Buson with a realistic description of nature, as advocated by Ōkyo, thus creating a fresh style. In this way were conceived the foundations for the enormously popular Shijō school, so named after Fourth Avenue in Kyoto, where Goshun's studio was located.

The woodcutters on the right screen and the fishermen on the left are all elderly men, who look more like wise men in exile than simple workmen. Here, Goshun's early aspiration as a Nanga painter is clearly expressed. He idealizes the simple existence of these men, far from worldly worries and in direct communication with nature. The vast emptiness where the two screens meet creates an illusion of widely separated worlds. Masses of foliage are composed of a multitude of tiny ink strokes united by pale washes of color.

Woodcutters and Fishermen (detail).

14. Autumn Millet

Edo period, early seventeenth century; attributed to Kanō Sanraku (1559–1635)
Pair of eight-fold screens; color on gilded paper; H. 38¾ in., W. 139½ in., each screen
Seals: "Shuri" and "Mitsuyori" on both screens
Published: Alan Priest, "Autumn Millet," *The Metropolitan Museum of Art Bulletin* 17 (December 1958), pp. 101–107
Lent by The Metropolitan Museum of Art; purchase, Pulitzer Bequest, 1957

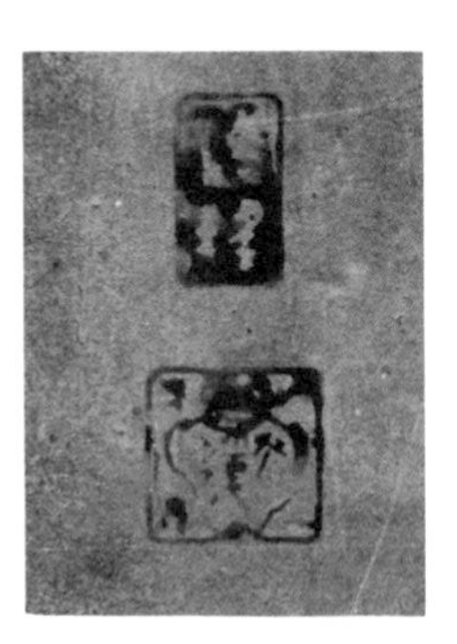

THE TIME is autumn. Millet grain is fully ripe and wild asters are in full bloom. Millet stalks and leaves, asters, and ragworts are swayed by gentle breezes. As finches, sparrows, and other birds flutter above the fence, the sky seems agitated. Some birds alight on ropes strung from bamboo poles. On the ground are quail and sparrows, picking the scattered grain. A sense of structural stability is created in the composition by a net and the parallel lines of bamboo fences, and by the curving ground line which cuts across both screens. Green leaves, rich red-brown grain, and pure white flowers stand forth against the gold ground.

The painting has four seals of Sanraku, who studied under Eitoku, and who was later allowed to use the Kanō name. The name Shuri appears in two rectangular seals, but the writing in the two larger seals, with cauldron shapes within squares, is indecipherable, although it is usually interpreted as Mitsuyori, a youthful name of Sanraku. These seals are found on almost all paintings attributed to him, but their presence alone does not insure his authorship. The screens, "Autumn Millet," may not be by Sanraku himself, but if not, they were probably painted by one of his close associates who followed his style faithfully.

Autumn Millet (detail).

15. Pheasants under Cherry and Willow Trees

Edo period, first half of the seventeenth century; attributed to Watanabe Ryōkei (d. 1645)
One of a pair of six-fold screens; color on gilded paper; H. 63 in., W. 143 ¼ in.
Published: *Zaigai Hihō* II, pl. 31
Lent by Mr. and Mrs. John D. Rockefeller 3rd

THIS SCREEN, showing pheasants and trees, originally formed a pair with its companion piece representing iris flowers in a pond. The screens were unfortunately separated, the iris screen now being in the collection of Joseph Brotherton in California.[1] If shown as a pair, the Rockefeller screen would stand at the right, and its large, scalloped cloud would continue into the iris screen.

The cherry blossoms are white and the young willow leaves a delicate green. Drooping willow branches almost touch the bright blue water. The colors are kept within the cool hues of blues and greens, with a slight touch of brown. Their fresh brilliance is accentuated by the gold background and white flowers.

The delicate and gentle fall of the willow branches recalls some screen paintings in the audience room at a temple in Kyoto, Nishi Honganji, which are attributed to Watanabe Ryōkei.[2] The life and works of this painter of the Kanō school were forgotten until recently. Tsugiyoshi Doi, who has rediscovered Ryōkei, attributes the Rockefeller screen also to him.[3] Although details of this painter's life are still obscure, a few facts are known. He was apparently of the Watanabe family, whose members were and still are the official painters for the temple of Nishi Honganji and for its abbots, members of the Ōtani family. A pupil of Kanō Mitsunobu (1565–1608), the eldest son of Eitoku (1543–1590), Ryōkei worked for temples in Kyoto, sometimes helping Mitsunobu or his colleague, Kōi (d. 1636). Ryōkei's works are found in a number of temples in the vicinity of Kyoto but are mainly concentrated in Nishi Honganji. The screen in the present exhibition was formerly in the Nishi Honganji collection, and it still has, on the reverse side, the painted design of half-raised bamboo blinds, the mark of the Ōtani family's possessions.

1. *Zaigai Hihō* II, pl. 32.
2. *Nishi Honganji, Shōheki-ga Zenshū* [Collection of Screen Paintings], vol. VI (Tokyo, 1968), pp. 113–125.
3. *Zaigai Hihō* II, pl. 31.

Pheasants under Cherry and Willow Trees (detail).

16. Fish Nets

Momoyama period; attributed to Kaihō Yūshō (1530–1615)
Pair of six-fold screens; color on gilded paper; H. 65¾ in., W. 150½ in., each screen
Published: "Aboshi Zu" [Drying Fishing Nets], *The Kokka*, no. 625 (December 1942), p. 375
Lent by The Brooklyn Museum of Art; C. H. DeSilver and E. C. Woodward Funds

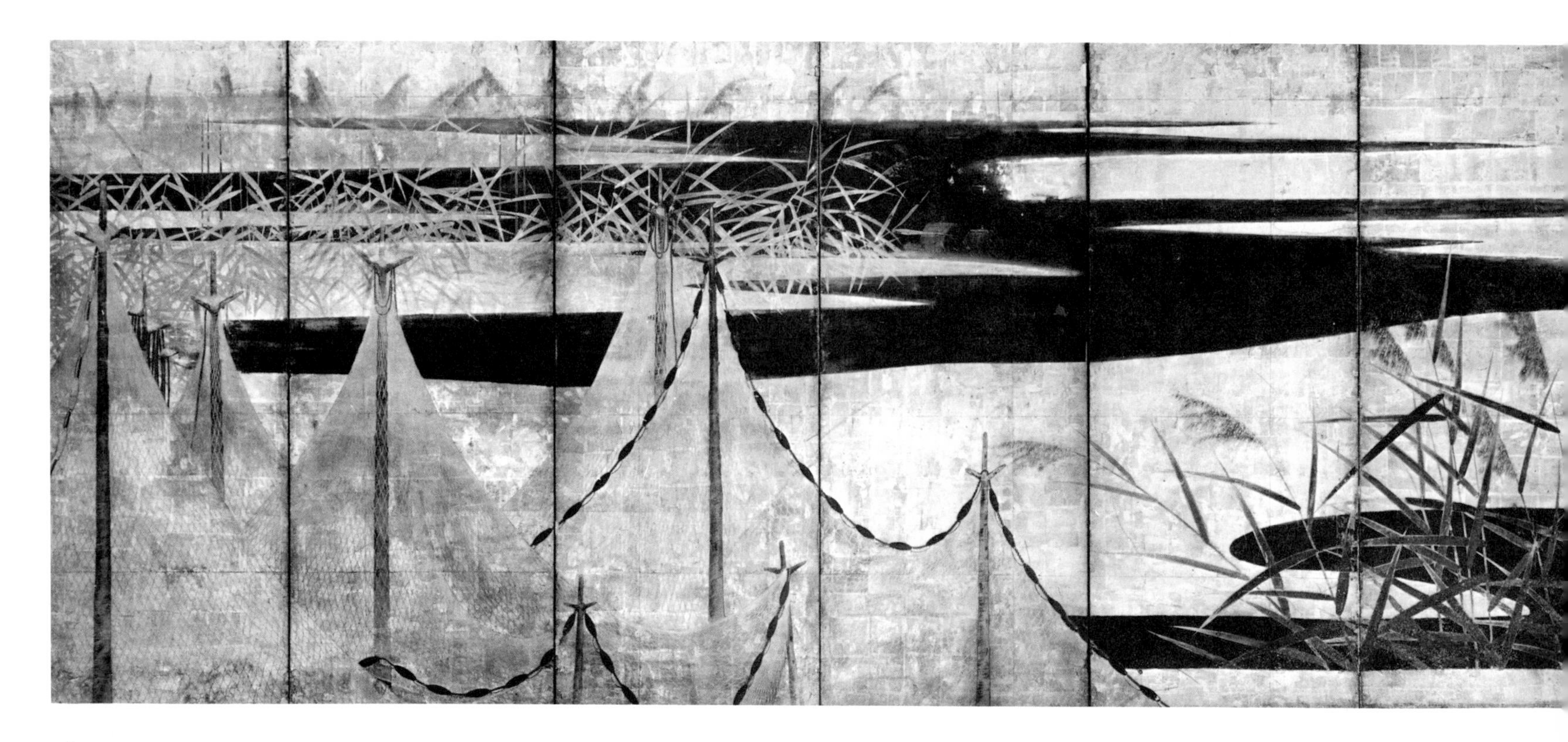

BANDS OF BRIGHT GOLD and dark blue in zigzag formation create a setting of sea and shore. Pyramidal shapes of fishing nets strung up on vertical poles pierce through the horizontal bands. The clash between opposing elements is somewhat softened by green reeds swaying in the wind, echoing the rhythmic lines of the nets. The painting is a superb example of typical Momoyama design which once filled the enormous rooms of palace and castle with its decorative splendor. At closer inspection, one realizes that there is in these screens a subtle but distinct illusion of changing seasons. Spring, when reeds are still young and small, appears in the extreme right panels; then comes summer, when the reeds grow larger and more sturdy, as shown in the left side of the right screen. The season of autumn, when the reeds turn to seed, is shown in the first panels of the left screen. Finally, in the upper left section, winter makes its appearance, and dry leaves falling to the frozen ground create a discordant note. The painter of these screens has realized all the exciting artistic potentialities of this simple subject in terms of a juxtaposition of triangles, verticals, and horizontals.

There are at least two more pairs of screens in Japanese collections that treat this subject, and all three versions look very much alike. Stylistically, they appear to derive from the hand of one artist, or at least one atelier, and traditionally they are attributed to Kaihō Yūshō. The only basis for this attribution is that one set, now in the Imperial Household collection, was once owned by Prince Katsura, who patronized Yūshō and who owned a pair of his landscape screens now in the Tokyo National Museum. Whatever the case, the creator of this painting was a master of ink technique, as superbly revealed in details of definition on the wood poles. He was also a great designer, who achieved dramatic splendor with the minimum of colors and forms.

Fish Nets (detail).

17. Cherry Trees

Momoyama period; Anonymous
Pair of six-fold screens; color on gilded paper; H. 69 in., W. 146 in., each screen
Published: Kōzō Sasaki, "Sakura Zu Byōbu" [Screens of Picture of Cherry Blossoms], *Kobijutsu*, no. 28 (December 1969), pp. 93, 94
Lent by Mr. and Mrs. Mathias Komor

MONUMENTAL CHERRY TREES spread their branches forcefully over these screens. Except for a few small, inconspicuous flowers at the lower left of the left screen, all subsidiary elements are eliminated, leaving only the old cherry trees of heroic size. Small white blossoms cling in clusters to slender, supple shoots, gracefully silhouetted against a brilliant gold cloud. The tree trunks and their branches disappear and reappear from behind the cloud, against a sky which is now the black of tarnished silver. One can only imagine what once must have been a brilliantly shining silver sky, when the foil was fresh. In these screens Momoyama design reaches its ultimate form, with a bold focus on a single motif demanding our undivided attention. The volume of the tree trunks is well defined by vertical and diagonal strokes in ink and touches of gold. The brush is carried swiftly, but with utmost assurance, to delineate the graceful growth of young branches.

The screens do not have a seal or signature, but they do have certain affinities with the works of Kaihō Yūshō. In painting trees and their branches, Yūshō often used vertical and diagonal lines in powerful ink strokes to create an effect of mass and volume. He also painted old trees with their young branches shooting upward in quick, sweeping movement, characteristics found in this pair of screens of the cherry trees, which may have been painted by one of his close associates or by a son.

Cherry Trees (detail).

18. Uji Bridge

Momoyama period; Anonymous
Pair of six-fold screens; color and gold on paper; H. 67 in., W. 136 in., each screen
Lent by Mr. and Mrs. Jackson Burke

Uji Bridge. Right screen.

THE PAINTING REPRESENTS the bridge over the Uji River in southeast Kyoto, one of the famous scenic views of Japan immortalized by many artists and poets. The place was dear to the Japanese of ancient times for its unforgettable beauty—the rolling hills in the surrounding areas, the clear water, and the splendid bridge. This painting belongs to the ancient tradition which found expression in depicting famous views of Japan in the four seasons. There are two archetypes for the subject of the Uji Bridge as it was represented on screens. In the earlier type, willow trees and the bridge are set against rolling hills and rice fields, and the seasons are clearly differentiated.[1] In the second type, represented by the screens in the Burke collection, the composition consists only of the bridge, willows, a water wheel, and baskets—in a design of utmost simplicity.

An enormous bridge in gold sweeps upward in a strong diagonal from the lower right corner of the right screen, continuing onto the left screen where it spans the upper half of the composition in a bold horizontal pattern. When the two screens stand slightly separated, their arrangement, in accordion shape, leads the eye in a zigzag movement, making the bridge seem even longer than it actually is. A crescent moon hanging in the sky, made of copper, is attached to the screen by small pegs. Three willow trees are placed at strategic points, at the right, middle, and left. Small, delicate leaves on the trees at right and center symbolize the spring season when new leaves have just emerged, while the fuller, longer leaves at the left suggest summer growth. Small, square pieces of gold are pasted on larger areas of gold that form irregularly shaped clouds. Gold is used abundantly. It has varying hues, so that light creates a subtle change of reflection. The water area is much darker now than it was originally, because the silver used on the waves has tarnished.

These screens with their dramatic contrasts of large forms and brilliant, shimmering hues of gold epitomize the Momoyama decorative style. Such compositions were extremely popular and in great demand. A number of versions exist in American and Japanese collections, almost all identical except for slight differences in detail and quality. Two versions are said to have the seals of Hasegawa Tōhaku,[2] noted painter of the Momoyama period; another has the seal of Hasegawa Sōya, reputedly the son of Tōhaku.[3] It is still premature to attribute all screens of the Uji Bridge to Hasegawa artists, but it is true that willows with long, slender leaves gently swaying in the breeze are found in many screen paintings by artists of this school. It may yet be proved that a Hasegawa artist composed the Burke screens.

1. Hiroshi Mizuo, "Uji-gawa Zu Byobū" [The Uji-gawa River], *The Kokka*, no. 873 (December 1964), pp. 23–31.

2. "Kyōryū Zu Byōbu Kai" [The Willows and a Bridge], *The Kokka*, no. 445 (December 1927), p. 337.

3. *Zaigai Hihō* II (Text), p. 17.

Uji Bridge (detail).

19. Tagasode (Whose Sleeves?)

Edo period, early seventeenth century; Anonymous
Six-fold screen; color on gilded paper; H. 67¼ in., W. 150 in.
Lent by Mr. and Mrs. Jackson Burke

THE TITLE of this painting, and of many others like it, is "Tagasode," meaning "whose sleeves?" The word "Tagasode" was used often in Japanese poems as the pillow-word—the word leading into a poem. A poem which begins with this word often implies a beautiful woman whose absence is missed. Beautiful sleeves, alluding to kimono, evoke the image of a beautiful woman; they also imply the fragrance of perfume arising from her kimono. Paintings which depict kimono may include a perfume bag, women's toys, musical instruments, or letter boxes; all are associated with the owner of kimono.

Two clothes racks laden with beautifully designed kimono are shown on the Burke screen: one in full view, and the other only in part. On the rack in the foreground, a tube containing an amulet is hung on a silken cord. At the foot of this rack is a *koto*. Both the furniture and the musical instrument are decorated with exquisite designs in gold; the rack in the background bears family emblems of almost identical size, suggesting that a pattern may have been used in drawing them. Many kimono represented in this painting have small tie-dyed designs, which may also have been stencilled, as they are uniform in size and regular in arrangement. Other designs, such as the half-wheels in the waves, bamboo stalks and maple leaves, or stylized waves are typical of fabric designs made in the first half of the seventeenth century.

The subject of Tagasode for painting seems to have developed as an abstraction of genre painting depicting beautiful women dressed in the latest fashion. As the emphasis on costumes increased, the figure itself became less important and was finally eliminated altogether. This theme, which only hints at the presence of a woman but refrains from portraying her, is typically Japanese. It is more evocative than the actual representation of a woman.

This subject enjoyed immense popularity during the late Momoyama—early Edo periods when many artists of various schools produced paintings to satisfy the demand. Some of these screens may be attributed to Sōtatsu and his atelier.[1] Kaihō Yūshō and his associates seem to have painted this theme too.[2] After the middle of the seventeenth century, however, the screens were replaced by scrolls showing single figures of women, or Ukiyo-e prints of the same subject, both of which were much less costly than screen paintings and appealed more directly to unsophisticated patrons.

1. *Zaigai Hiho* II, pl. 49.
2. Tanio Nakamura, "Tagasode Byōbu" [A Folding-Screen Picture Called *Tagasode*], *The Kokka*, no. 804 (March 1959) pp. 84–91.

Tagasode (*Whose Sleeves?*) (detail).

20. The Tales of the Hōgen and Heiji Insurrections

Momoyama period, late sixteenth century; Anonymous
Pair of six-fold screens; color and gold on paper; H. 67½ in., W. 147 in., each screen
Published: *Zaigai Hihō* II, pl. 18. Miyeko Murase, "Japanese Screen Paintings of the Hōgen and Heiji Insurrections," *Artibus Asiae* 29, nos. 2/3 (January 1967), pp. 193–228. "Hōgen Heiji Kassen Zu Byōbu Kai" [The Wars of Hōgen and Heiji], *The Kokka*, no. 519 (February 1934), pp. 36–44.
Lent by The Metropolitan Museum of Art; Rogers Fund, 1957

Right screen, Hōgen.

FOLLOWING PAGES: *The Tales of the Hōgen and Heiji Insurrections*; Hōgen (details).

THE TWO CIVIL WARS that occurred in the Hōgen and Heiji eras took place in 1156 and 1159, respectively. The fighting lasted only a few days in each case and it involved merely a handful of politically eminent men of the Heike (also known as Taira) and Genji (also known as Minamoto) clans. Yet, historically speaking, these are two of the most memorable insurrections of medieval Japan; they signaled the collapse of an old order and the coming of a new era. Blood-curdling incidents of these two wars, mixed with romantic interludes, became the basis for the first historical war novels of Japan, the *Hōgen Monogatari* (Tale of the Hōgen Incident) and the *Heiji Monogatari*[1] (Tale of the Heiji Incident). The *Hōgen Monogatari* focuses on the decline of the once supremely powerful Fujiwara aristocrats, and the rise of the two military families, the Genji and the Heike. The *Heiji Monogatari*, on the other hand, describes the jealousy and the inevitable conflicts between these two warrior clans, and a temporary defeat of the Minamoto family.

Both stories were illustrated in narrative scroll paintings (*emaki*) in the Kamakura period, but only small portions of the scrolls depicting the Heiji War survive today. One scroll out of the set of the Heiji pictures now belongs to the Museum of Fine Arts in Boston, and is popularly known as the scroll of the "Burning of the Sanjō Palace."[2] As for the pictures of the Kamakura period depicting the Hōgen Incident, all are lost and we know of their existence only through literary references. The screens in the Metropolitan Museum are the oldest extant examples of painting which represent both the Hōgen and Heiji wars. The dark greens, browns, and blues of the landscape, sharply contrasted against scattered clouds of brilliant gold create colorful and decorative effects. The entire city of Kyoto, where the major military actions took place, is viewed from above, and its vast panorama opens before us. Mountains, rivers, houses, and hundreds of men and women emerge from behind the scalloped gold clouds. Warriors swarm around palatial buildings, or are engaged in fierce battles on the streets and river banks. They are short-necked, strong-jawed, bearded men of action. Their uncouth character and low station in life are clearly expressed in their faces.

The most important military actions are depicted in the central areas of both screens, while the prologues and epilogues of the battles are scattered at the edges. There is no chronological sequence in the arrangement of episodes. The city and its suburbs seem to have been laid out first, and only later were the historical episodes fitted into every nook and corner of mountains, city streets, and buildings. For example, the first episode in the Hōgen Incident, the death of the Emperor Konoe in 1155, which was the direct cause of the war, is illustrated at the bottom of the fifth panel in the Hōgen screen (the right screen). The event immediately following this episode is shown in the lower part of the fourth panel, separated by a few scenes.

The most dramatic episode of the Heiji War is undoubtedly the burning of the Sanjō Palace. On the Heiji screen (the left screen), this story is depicted in the central area, spanning the third and fourth panels. There is a skirmish going on in the house across from the Kamo River, towards the upper right; this is the Rokuhara Mansion of Taira Kiyomori, leader of the Heike. The mansion is surrounded by fighting soldiers. On the verandah stands a man who is recognizable as Kiyomori himself. He is represented in the picture as he is described in legend, having placed his helmet backwards on his head, so frightened was he by the enemy's battle cry. Also depicted is another equally well-known episode of this novel, which took place twenty-one years after the battles of 1159. Yoritomo, of the temporarily defeated Minamoto clan, who was later to become the first shogun of Japan, finally found his opportunity to take revenge on the Taira family. Mt. Fuji, the scene of this later battle, rises suddenly above the rivers and mountains at the top of the fifth panel. In the dark of night, in 1180, Yoritomo confronted the Heike troops at the foot of this beautiful mountain. Even before his army made a move, however, his opponents were frightened by a flock of water birds, and fled without shooting a single arrow. The white, snow-capped mountain rising high above the golden clouds is like an auspicious symbol of the forthcoming brilliant career of Yoritomo, who later emerged as the uncontested ruler of Japan.

Judging from the details of the palace architecture and the style of the figures, the screens may be attributed to a Tosa artist of the late sixteenth century, in the Momoyama period.[3]

Many scenes in these screens are very similar to the fan paintings made after these stories by Sōtatsu and his associates in the seventeenth century,[4] and they offer interesting information on the work habits of Sōtatsu's studio.

1. Some portions of these Tales are translated: E. R. Kellog, "The Hōgen Monogatari," *Transactions of the Asiatic Society of Japan* 45 (September 1917), pp. 25–117; K. Florenz, *Geschichte der japanischen Litteratur* (Leipzig, 1906), pp. 294–298; E. O. Reischauer and K. Yamagiwa, *Translations from Early Japanese Literature* (Cambridge, Mass., 1951), pp. 396–446.
2. *Heiji Monogatari Emaki, Nihon Emaki-mono Zenshū* [Japanese Scroll Paintings], vol. IX (Tokyo, 1964).
3. Murase, *op. cit.*, pp. 206–228.
4. Yamane, *Sōtatsu*, pp. 60–78.

The Tales of the Hōgen and Heiji Insurrections; Hōgen (detail).

The Tales of the Hōgen and Heiji Insurrections. Left screen, Heiji.
FOLLOWING PAGES: *The Tales of the Hōgen and Heiji Insurrections*; Heiji (details).

21. Biography of Priest Saigyō

Momoyama period, late sixteenth century; Anonymous
Pair of six-fold screens; color and gold on paper; H. 66½ in., W. 147 in., each screen
Published: Yoshi Shirahata, "Saigyō Monogatari Byōbu" [Screens Illustrating Biography of Priest Saigyō], *Kobijutsu*, no. 5 (August 1964), pp. 103–107
Lent by Mr. and Mrs. Jackson Burke

SAIGYŌ, a warrior-turned-poet, is one of the greatest and most beloved poets of Japan.[1] Saigyō (1118–ca. 1190), was known as Satō Norikiyo when he was a promising junior officer at the court. At the age of twenty-six, however, he resigned from his post and renounced his wife and a four-year-old daughter in the hope of finding peace as a wandering monk-poet. To abandon this earthly world and enter the priesthood to seek union with god and nature through travel—this was the dream of every educated man of Japan during the Heian and Kamakura periods. Saigyō's brave decision and subsequent life appealed to many Japanese. He was a great poet as well, and his poems, composed during his wanderings, became popular in medieval Japan.

It is to be expected that the life of such a man should become a subject for painting, and indeed, the earliest extant picture illustrating his biography was made in the first half of the thirteenth century, not long after his death.[2] Perhaps the whole set of this thirteenth-century painting consisted of four scrolls, but only two scrolls remain today: one in the Tokugawa Museum in Nagoya and the other in the Ōhara collection in Okayama. The subject remained a favorite among painters throughout the Muromachi and Edo periods. In 1500, Kaida Unume painted an *emaki* of Saigyō's life. Copies of this scroll made by Sōtatsu in 1630 survive in two versions, one in the Watanabe collection, and the other in the Morikawa collection.[3]

The screens in the Burke collection are based on this long tradition. They are in unusually good condition, the gold squares and flakes shimmering in still fresh hues. The dense green of hills and the bright red of the mountain shrine stand out vividly against the glitter of golden clouds. The sharp edges of the gold foil are tastefully camouflaged by a liberal sprinkling of small flakes of gold which add luster and give the clouds a vaporous quality. Illustrated on the right screen is the episode of Saigyō celebrating the first New Year's Day after leaving his post, his friends, and his family. Alone in a room at the left of the screen, he gazes outward at the prized white plum blossoms of early spring. In the adjoining rooms children and priests enjoy the quiet leisure of the holiday, some by playing a game of *go* while others study a Buddhist sutra. These scenes are identical to those represented in the Ōhara collection's scroll of the thirteenth century.

On the left screen are depicted episodes from Saigyō's wanderings in the area south of Nara, where he went in search of early cherry blossoms. While traveling from Yoshino to Kumano over the mountain path he happened to see some beautiful cherry blossoms at a small mountain shrine, Yagami Ōji, These blossoms looked especially fragile and lovely against the green leaves and brilliant red of the Shinto shrine. In the upper left area of this screen we see Saigyō, overcome with joy, as he composed a poem and wrote it on the wooden fence of the shrine:

> Long-awaited cherries of Yagami are finally
> in bloom,
> Oh, the wind and breezes over the mountains
> and pine trees,
> Do not come down hard on these fragile flowers.[4]

At the bottom of this screen is a scene of parting. Saigyō had met and traveled for a few days with mendicant monks who became good friends of the poet. Now they were forced to part, and the scene shows the two monks weeping and bidding him farewell. Four cows at the left seem unaware of the sorrowful occasion. Except for these animals, whose positions differ from those in the *emaki* in the Ōhara collection, the scenes on the screen and in the scroll are identical.

Undoubtedly the artist who painted these screens had had an opportunity to study, and copy, the thirteenth-century *emaki*. Here he has tried to recapture not only the scenes but also some of the flavor of the thirteenth-century scroll painting. He has imitated the soft, vaporous quality of the clouds in the early *emaki* with a sprinkling of gold flakes. Small slivers of silver, simulating fallen pine needles, are scattered on the ground, creating decorative patterns like those found frequently in paintings of the Fujiwara and Kamakura periods. The artist seems to have greatly admired the ancient paintings of Japan. He probably belonged to the Tosa school, which more than any other most faithfully maintained the traditional techniques.

1. Robert G. Sewell, "A Study of Saigyō with Translation of His Poems in the Shinkokinshū" (Master's Essay, Columbia University, 1967).
2. *Saigyō Monogatari Emaki, Nihon Emaki-mono Zenshū*, vol. XI (Tokyo, 1958).
3. Yamane, *Sōtatsu*, pp. 177–185; Teiji Chizawa, *Sōtatsu, Nihon no Bijutsu* [Arts of Japan], ed. National Museums of Tokyo, Kyoto, and Nara, vol. XXXI (Tokyo, 1968).
4. *Saigyō Monogatari Emaki*, pl. 47.

22. Rakuchū-Rakugai (Inside and Outside of Kyoto)

Edo period, first half of the seventeenth century; Anonymous
Pair of six-fold screens; color on gilded paper; H. 68½ in., W. 147 in., each screen
Lent by The Brooklyn Museum of Art; gift of Mr. W. W. Hoffman

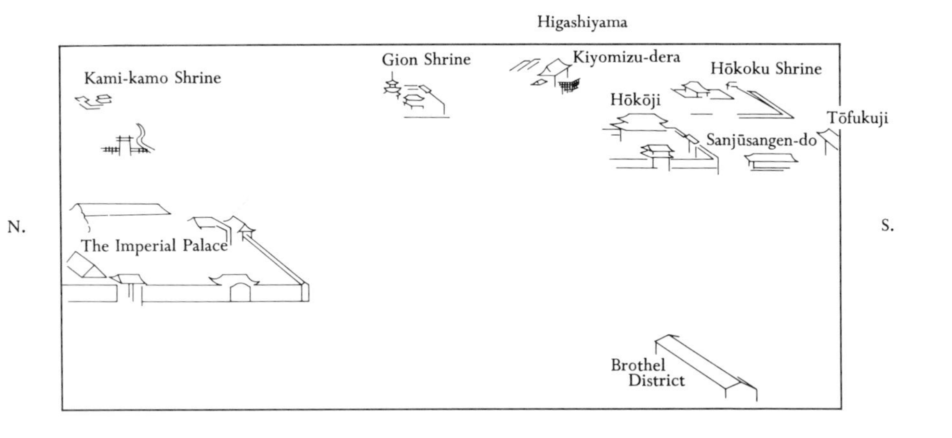

Right screen.

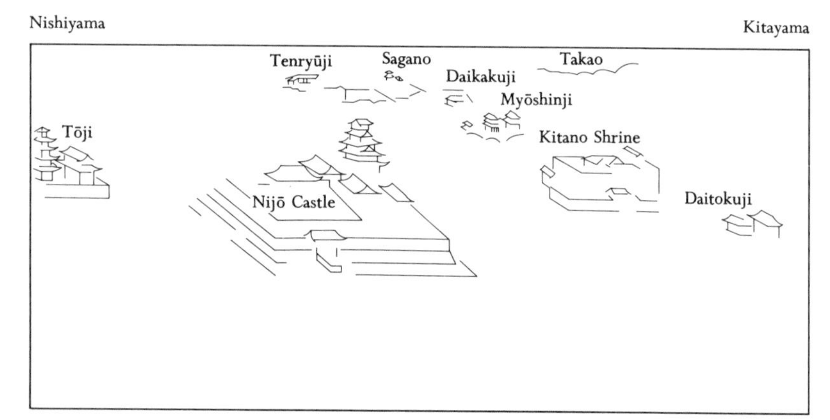
Nishiyama
Kitayama
Tenryūji
Sagano
Takao
Daikakuji
Myōshinji
Tōji
Kitano Shrine
Nijō Castle
Daitokuji
S.
N.

Rakuchū-Rakugai (Inside and Outside of Kyoto). Left screen.

PAINTINGS DEPICTING VIEWS of Kyoto and its suburbs are known in Japan as Rakuchū-Rakugai Zu—*rakuchū* (capital's inside), *rakugai* (capital's outside), *zu* (pictures). The word "*raku*," meaning a capital, is the Japanese pronunciation of the first Chinese character in the name "Loyang," the city in northeast China which was frequently chosen as the capital of ancient China. Rakuchū-Rakugai pictures represent the final development of the native themes of Famous Views and Four Seasons. These views of Kyoto, which are usually painted on screens, illustrate famous scenic spots and important monuments of the capital and its suburbs which served as settings for seasonal festivals and entertainments. Such screens were much admired and in great demand among the people of Kyoto, and also among out-of-town visitors who bought them eagerly as souvenirs of their trips to the capital. One of the two earliest extant screens of this type was acquired on just such an occasion: Oda Nobunaga gave a pair of screens with this subject to Lord Uesugi as a going-away gift. The screens were painted by Eitoku, then a young man; they are still in the possession of descendants of Lord Uesugi.

Artists who painted the Kyoto screens usually had a keen sense of history; they recorded buildings, monuments, customs—and changes in them—with archaeological accuracy. Details of this sort often help to date the screens; they also aid the study of the physical and cultural aspects of the ancient capital. Within these paintings are scenes which later became prototypes for independent genre subjects such as the Kabuki theatre, the Kamo horse race, the archery contest at Sanjūsangen-dō, maple-viewing and cherry blossom-viewing parties (No. 23), the Gion Festival, and scenes in the brothel districts (No. 25).

In 1503 Tosa Mitsunobu (d. ca. 1523) painted one screen showing views of only the inner capital, *rakuchū*. It was regarded at that time as a novelty.[1] A prototype for the Rakuchū-Rakugai pictures seems to have been established shortly afterwards. The oldest extant screens of this type are a pair in the Machida collection (ca. 1521–1525)[2] and the pair mentioned above, in the Uesugi collection (ca. 1550's–1560's).[3] They follow a standard composition which may be considered as the first stage in the development of this genre. The city of Kyoto is divided into two sections, the left screen showing views of the uptown district, the right one the downtown district.

The screens in the Brooklyn Museum are typical of the second stage of this development. The city is now divided into eastern and western halves, with Abura-kōji street (running east of Nijō Castle) as the dividing line. On the right screen is shown the eastern half of the city with its hills (Higashiyama), and the Gion Festival is the dominant theme. On the left screen are Nijō Castle and the western half of the city, with the northern hills (Kitayama) and the western hills (Nishiyama).

A word must be said here to guide the viewer to the correct orientation of the screens. When the two screens are unfolded for view, they should not be placed side by side; rather, they should face each other, flanking the viewer. When this is done, south is at the right side of the right screen, and north is at its left side; on the facing (left) screen, north is at the right side of the screen, and south at the left. Scenes of the Four Seasons are frequently included in these screens. Contrary to the usual practice of depicting winter in the extreme left panels of the left screen, in these, winter now appears at the top right-hand corner of the left screen. This location is a logical one since on the Rakuchū-Rakugai screens it represents the northern hill section, an appropriate place for winter scenery.

On the Brooklyn screens a panoramic view of the city with houses, temples, shrines, and palaces opens before us. Buildings, trees, and human figures emerge from beneath golden clouds decorated with patterns in relief. City streets and houses are laid out in an orderly, well-organized scheme, an effect achieved by subordinating the human figures and their activities. In fact, the only action of major importance depicted on the screens is the Gion Festival procession, which takes place in mid-July. A major tourist attraction even today, this festival originated in the mid-ninth century and has been observed annually with almost no interruption since 970. Here, shopkeepers, and pedestrians alike have deserted their homes and shops to watch the procession, with its colorful floats and theatrical performances, meandering through almost every street and avenue of the city. Even the brothel district (in the lower sections of the second panel of the right screen) seems deserted.

Rakuchū-Rakugai
Right screen.
(detail).

Rakuchū-Rakugai
Left screen.
(detail).

The general affluence of the citizens is apparent in the form of their houses, many of which are two-storied, some having tall, white-washed warehouses in their courtyards.

The most important monument on the right screen is the Imperial Palace, seen at the left. There is no other building of consequence in the eastern section of the inner city. For other well-known monuments, we must turn to the suburbs on the eastern hills, represented on the upper section of the screen.

Among the better-known Buddhist temples in this section, starting from the south (right-hand side), are Tōfukuji; Sanjūsangen-dō, where a Sumō wrestling match is drawing the attention of on-lookers; and adjoining this the Great Buddha Hall of Hōkōji, which was dedicated by Toyotomi Hideyoshi in 1591. Moving slightly upward we come to another monument to the Toyotomi family, the Hōkoku Shrine, built as a mausoleum for Hideyoshi in 1599, a year after his death. To the north (left) of this shrine is the temple of Kiyomizu-dera, easily recognized by its high stilts; the Gion Shrine; and finally, at the top left the Kami-kamo Shrine, where the famous horse race customarily held on May 5, introduced in 678, is in progress. Throughout the eastern hills, pinkish white cherry blossoms dot valleys and rises. Spring is depicted in the suburbs of Kyoto, but in the city proper and at Kami-kamo summer festivals reign.

On the left screen, the seasons are somewhat mingled. The mid-July Gion Festival procession and floats continue onto this screen, passing before Nijō Castle. Yet, on the upper section of the screen, where the western and northern hills are represented, blazing red maple leaves signal autumn, and at the top right-hand corner, some hills are covered with snow.

Nijō Castle, the major monument in the western section of the city, occupies the central area of this screen. This palace-castle was completed in 1603 as Shogun Ieyasu's temporary residence in Kyoto, and underwent an extensive renovation in 1626. The new *tenshukaku* (keep), added at that time, is represented in the painting as slightly separated from the main cluster of palace buildings by a scalloped cloud; this arrangement reflects the actual appearance of the castle after the renovation of 1626 and thus provides a *terminus post quem* for the painting. Other notable monuments and temples of the west side are concentrated in the suburbs. Starting at the right (north), they are: Daitokuji; the Kitano Shrine; Takao, the favorite maple-viewing place, directly above it; Myōshinji; and Daikakuji. Some women are husking rice near Shakadō in the Sagano district. Tenryūji is located near a large lake; near the top left is a river, where some fishermen are at work. Below the river is Tōji, with its five-storied pagoda, overlooking the city.

One clue to the date of these screens is provided by the renovations of Nijō Castle, as we noted above, and there is further evidence from other sources for a date in the first half of the seventeenth century. In the painting, the Hōkoku Shrine is represented as being in splendid condition and attracting many pilgrims. A few years after 1619, however, when the Tokugawa family issued a ban on any future repairs on this monument, the building was left to decay; its dilapidated condition drew laments from authors writing about Kyoto in the mid-seventeenth century.[4] As further evidence, the red-light district represented on the right screen in the downtown section of the east side was moved to its modern location, Shimabara, on the west side of the city, in 1641. These screens, therefore, should be dated between 1626 and 1641.

The Brooklyn screens have many features in common with a pair of screens in the Okayama Museum,[5] likewise dated in the early seventeenth century. In both sets of screens the city is viewed from the same vantage point, and the general layout of the city, its streets, suburbs, and also certain buildings, are alike. One notable difference between these screens is that the Okayama pair is more complex, involving many more monuments, events, and people. Certain stylistic features such as the brush strokes delineating landscape details, and the golden clouds with designs in relief, as well as the figurative types—short, chubby men and women with youthful, charming faces—suggest that the work was done in the Tosa atelier.

1. *Sanetaka-kō Ki* [Diary of Lord Sanjōnishi Sanetaka], ed. Zoku Gunsho Ruijū Kansei-kai, vol. IV, pt. 2 (Tokyo, 1961), p. 675, in the entry for December 22 of the third year of the Eishō era (1506).
2. Kyoto National Museum, ed., *Rakuchū Rakugai Zu* (Tokyo, 1966), color pls. 1, 2, black and white pl. 1.
3. *Ibid.*, color pl. 3, black and white pls. 2, 3.
4. *Ibid.*, p. 47.
5. *Ibid.*, color pl. 8, black and white pls. 10, 11.

23. Cherry-Blossom Viewing

Edo period, first half of the seventeenth century; Anonymous
Originally in two panels, now remounted into a single panel; color on gilded paper; H. 40 1/16 in., W., 73 1/8 in.
Published: Ichitarō Kondō, *Japanese Genre Painting* (Tokyo, 1961), no. 85. Tokyo National Museum, ed., *Japanese Genre Painting of the Early Modern Periods (Mid-Sixteenth to Early Eighteenth Centuries)* [Kinsei Shoki Fūzoku Ga] (Tokyo 1957), no. 44
Lent by Mr. and Mrs. Earl Morse

CHERRY BLOSSOMS are in full bloom, and merry parties are in progress before a Shinto shrine and a pagoda as citizens of Kyoto gather to enjoy this beautiful yet evanescent flowering. A young lord with many retainers is arriving from the right. Tea is being served in the tea house in the lower right corner, while two fashionably dressed ladies playing a game of *go* appear within another tea house. The merriest party occupies a temporary enclosure, at the upper left of the panel, consisting of a folding screen and a curtain of fine fabrics hanging from a rope. Within, a woman dances to the accompaniment of *shamisen* (a three-stringed instrument with a long neck) and *koto*. Near the pagoda, a cook is preparing a large fish, while customers watch him with an expression of serious concern. At the Shinto shrine a young maiden rings the bell to petition the god. Looking on with curiosity is a Chinese visitor wearing a tall hat and accompanied by a Japanese guide. A feeling of gaiety and carefree pleasure, without rowdiness, pervades the scene.

Cherry-blossom viewing at a picnic, a favorite pastime of the Japanese, ancient and modern alike, provided an indispensable subject for Japanese painting from ancient times. In traditional paintings of the Four Seasons spring was represented by a scene of cherry-blossom viewing, while in paintings of the scenes of the calendar year the month of March was so illustrated. Cherry-viewing picnics often took place in the compounds of Buddhist temples or Shinto shrines, where splendid blossoms were to be seen. The gaiety at these merry parties would remind the citizens of the promised paradise of Buddha. Pilgrimages to sacred monuments, therefore, often included cherry-viewing parties; thus profane pleasure was elevated to the level of a sacred experience.

In the Momoyama and Edo periods, the Higashiyama (eastern hills) district of Kyoto was singled out as the most popular cherry-blossom viewing place because of its profusion of beautiful flowers. The area included places such as the Gion Shrine, the Yasaka Shrine, and Kiyomizu-dera. The Shinto shrine with a Buddhist pagoda in this painting may be the Gion Shrine since it resembles this popular Shinto monument as represented in many paintings.

Exquisite details in the rendering of the costumes and of the delicate white cherry blossoms, and a refined sensitivity in the choice of colors characterize this painting. Contemporary life is reflected in the fashions in dress, objects such as the *shamisen*, which gained popularity ca. 1614, tobacco smoking, fashionable at this time, and the little Portuguese dog of a type introduced in the early seventeenth century.

Like so many other genre paintings, this one has neither seal nor signature. It was probably painted by an artist employed by a shop which sold ready-made pictures of this type. The figures of tall, slender men and women with rather long, full faces resemble the type frequently painted by Kanō artists in the second quarter of the seventeenth century. Strong ink strokes in the landscape details also suggest that the artist was trained in the Kanō school.

Cherry-Blossom Viewing (detail).

24. Noh and Kyōgen Plays

Edo period, seventeenth century; Anonymous
Six-fold screen; color and gold on paper; H. 32¼ in., W. 99 in.
Published: *Zaigai Hihō* III, pl. 7
Lent by Mr. Martin Carr

THREE NOH PLAYS and three Kyōgen (farcical interludes) are depicted alternately on this six-panel screen. Pictures showing Noh dramas are frequently represented in large screen paintings such as Rakuchū-Rakugai, which include illustrations of various entertainment districts. Pictures of Noh plays, however, never attained the same degree of popularity as those of the Kabuki theatre. Screens such as this, devoted entirely to the representation of episodes from the Noh drama, were rare, whereas Kabuki scenes often appeared independently as the subject matter on screens. This is an unusual work also because of its format, which recalls that of ancient folding screens; each of its six panels, surrounded by a wide border, is treated as a distinct unit.

The first panel, counting from the right, represents a Noh drama entitled *Tōru*. The ghost of the dead minister Tōru appears on a moonlit night at the ruin of his once sumptuous mansion; he reminisces to a traveling monk about his brilliant career.[1] The second panel depicts a Kyōgen, *Fukurō* (an owl). A young man has contracted a strange illness and he now speaks with the voice of an owl. His brother calls for a mendicant monk to cure him. But they, too, are stricken by the same disease, and all three talk in owl-like voices. The third panel shows a Noh play which is based on a tragic episode from chapter nine of the *Tale of Genji*. A group of people is frightened by an apparition of the jealous Rokujō, Genji's much older mistress who killed Princess Aoi, his first wife.[2] On the fourth panel another Kyōgen is pictured, *Buaku* (a wild man). A lord wanted Buaku killed, but the latter safely escaped. Later, the two accidentally meet, and Buaku pretends that he is the dead spirit of himself. The last Noh play, depicted on the fifth panel, is called *Kumasaka*. This is one of many stories relating to the boyhood of Minamoto Yoshitsune, a tragic hero and a younger brother of Yoritomo, who became the first shogun of Japan. The ghost of a warrior, Kumasaka Naganori, appears and he re-enacts the situation in which he was defeated and killed by young Yoshitsune.[3] The sixth panel illustrates a Kyōgen known as *Kaki-yamabushi* (a persimmon-monk). A mendicant monk steals persimmons. He is tricked by the owner of the persimmon tree into pretending that he can fly like a bird; he falls off the tree. In revenge, he tries to place a curse on the owner of the tree.

Fine, delicate brush strokes define the elongated figures of dancers, spectators, and young musicians, some dressed in colorful costumes. The miniature ink paintings that decorate the screens shown upon the stages are executed with the same refinement. A quiet color scheme dominated by brown is quite appropriate for the hushed silence of the Noh theatre, interrupted only by the sounds of music and dance. In view of these characteristics, the screen may be attributed to a Tosa artist of the first half of the seventeenth century.

1. Murakami Upton, *A Spectator's Handbook of Noh* (Tokyo, 1963), pp. 72, 73.

2. Arthur Waley, *The Nō Plays of Japan* (New York, 1922), pp. 143–152.

3. *Ibid.*, pp. 59–68.

Noh and Kyōgen Plays (detail).

25. Entertainments at the House of Pleasure

Edo period, late seventeenth century; Anonymous
One of a pair of six-fold screens; color on gilded paper; H. 27⅝ in., W. 105½ in.
Lent by Mr. and Mrs. John G. Powers

AN AFTERNOON of lively merriment is in progress at an elegant house with a beautiful pond in its garden. In front of the gate at the right, sedan-chair carriers watch a Sumō wrestling match while waiting for their customers. In the courtyard a group of smartly dressed young men dance in a circle to the music played by an old blind musician. Excitement and disturbances are caused by a fat, unruly customer reclining on the verandah. Several fashionably dressed youths are quietly reading books, conversing, or fishing, while upstairs a man is aiming a gun at ducks in the lake. Vivid colors and lively activities create an impression of singing, laughter, and cries of delight, filling the screen with gaiety and sensuous pleasure.

This screen illustrates scenes at a house of pleasure, one of the subjects of the genre paintings known as Ukiyo-e which attained great popularity in the mid-seventeenth century. The screen in the present exhibition, which depicts a house of male prostitutes, forms a pair with another, also in the Powers collection, representing scenes at a house of female prostitutes. Pictures illustrating merry parties inside the house may be traced to the earlier pictorial type depicting outdoor picnic scenes, the earliest extant example of which is ''Maple Viewing at Takao'' (in the Tokyo National Museum) from the Muromachi period. Pictures of outdoor entertainments usually involve many groups in festive spirits, and large crowds of people scattered in wide landscape settings. However, there was a gradual shift from large, all-inclusive outdoor scenes to more limited and intimate views of indoor amusements, which demand careful and close scrutiny. In the pictures of indoor scenes, more emphasis is placed on individual figures of men and women, and on their beautifully designed clothing.

As in the case of many other early Ukiyo-e paintings, this screen is not signed. Ink paintings on the screens pictured within the house reveal the artist's familiarity with and competence in this medium. He was equally adept at describing nature in a delicate, colorful style, as is evident in the landscape scene at the left. The artist, who was trained in the Tosa school, painted this screen in the late seventeenth century.

Entertainments at the House of Pleasure (detail).

26. Taking Shelter from Rain

Edo period, eighteenth century; by Hanabusa Itchō (1652–1724)
Six-fold screen; color and ink on paper; H. 47¾ in., W. 124½ in.
Signature: "Hanabusa Itchō egaku"; Seals: "Shuzai San-un Senseki Kan" and "Ai Moko"
Published: Nobuo Tsuji, "Ama Yadori Zu" [Taking Shelter from Rain], *The Kokka*, no. 920 (November 1968), p. 35
Lent by Mr. and Mrs. Jackson Burke

A GROUP OF passers-by takes shelter from a sudden downpour. Heavy rain clouds envelop the roof tops, while the leaves of the trees tremble in the wind. At the right is a creek, already flooded, and wild grasses bend down, heavy with dew. Four men and a bamboo vendor are rushing towards the wide-eaved gate of a large estate. There, men and women of different classes and trades are already huddled together under the roof—a warrior, pilgrims, and a lion-dance performer, as well as a flower vendor and other tradesmen. A child grips a beam, hanging from it upside down; he alone seems quite unconcerned with the inconvenience of the weather. At the smaller gate to the left more men and women cluster together. Swallows flutter around the large tree, as if agitated by the storm. Light washes of color and fluid brush strokes in soft ink convey the wetness and the sudden coolness of the atmosphere.

The subject is a true genre theme, but focuses on commonplace people and their ways of life rather than on the gay quarters and theatre districts of Kyoto and Edo. Hanabusa Itchō seems to have chosen this subject as representative of summertime activities. His handscroll in the Honolulu Academy of Art, depicting activities of the calendar year, includes an almost identical scene for the month of June.[1] He seems to have been especially fond of this subject, as he used it again on a very similar screen which is now in the collection of Mr. and Mrs. John G. Powers.

Itchō first studied with Kanō Yasunobu (1618–1685), one of the leading masters of the Kanō family. For unknown reasons, he was soon expelled; he then studied haiku with Bashō (1644–1694), pursuing this art in great earnest and publishing a collection of his own poetry. He admired the paintings of the Ukiyo-e school, which was then rapidly gaining popularity, and tried to imitate the style of Hishikawa Moronobu (d. 1694). For reasons still unknown, Itchō was arrested in 1698 and sent into exile in Miyake-jima, an island south of Edo, where he spent twelve years before his release in 1709. Since he adopted the name Itchō only after his return from exile, the painting in the Burke collection, with the signature reading "Itchō," must be dated after that time.

1. *Zaigai Hihō* III (Text), p. 45.

Taking Shelter from Rain (detail).

Bibliography

AKIYAMA, TERUKAZU. *Japanese Painting* (Lausanne, 1961).

COVELL, JON C. *Masterpieces of Japanese Screen Painting, the Momoyama Period (Late Sixteenth Century)* (New York, 1962).

DOI, TSUGIYOSHI. *Momoyama no Shōheki-ga* [Screen Paintings of the Momoyama Period], *Nihon no Bijutsu* [Arts of Japan], vol. XIV (Tokyo, 1967).

————. *Momoyama Shōheki-ga no Kanshō* [Appreciation of the Momoyama Screen Paintings] (Tokyo, 1943).

————. *Shōheki-ga* [Screen Paintings], *Nihon Rekishi Shinsho* [New Series on Japanese History] (Tokyo, 1966).

GRILLI, ELISE. *The Art of the Japanese Screen* (Tokyo, 1970).

MAYUYAMA, JUNKICHI, ed. *Japanese Art in the West* (Tokyo, 1966).

MINAMOTO, HŌSHŪ, ed. *Momoyama Byōbu Taikan* [Screens of the Momoyama Period] (Kyoto, 1931).

NOMA, SEIROKU. *The Arts of Japan*, vol. II, *Late Medieval to Modern*, (Tokyo, 1967).

————, ed. *Momoyama Jidai no Meiga Shū* [Masterpieces of Paintings, Momoyama Period] (Tokyo, n.d.).

PAINE, R. T. *Catalogue of a Special Exhibition of Japanese Screen Paintings: Birds, Flowers and Animals, from the Collection in the Museum of Fine Arts, Boston* (Boston, 1935).

————. *Catalogue of a Special Exhibition of Japanese Screen Paintings: Landscapes and Figures from the Collection in the Museum of Fine Arts, Boston* (Boston, 1938).

PAINE, R. T. and SOPER, A. C. *The Art and Architecture of Japan* (Baltimore, 1955).

SANSOM, GEORGE. *A History of Japan*, 3 vols. (Stanford, 1958–1963).

SHIMADA, SHŪJIRŌ, ed. *Zaigai Hihō* [Japanese Paintings in Western Collections], 3 vols. (Tokyo, 1969).

TAKEDA, TSUNEO. *Shōheki-ga* [Screen Paintings], *Genshoku Nihon no Bijutsu* [Japanese Arts in Colors], vol. XIII (Tokyo, n.d.).

TOKYO NATIONAL MUSEUM, ed. *Momoyama Jidai Shōheki-ga Zu-shū* [Collection of Momoyama Period Door and Screen Paintings] (Tokyo, 1929).

Catalogue designed by Joseph Bourke Del Valle.

Production supervised by Françoise J. Boas.

All color photographs are by Otto E. Nelson and all black and white photographs with the exception of the following: number 8 by William Pons; number 9 by Eric Politzer; number 11 by Helga Photo Studio Inc.; number 12 by Richard Taylor; number 20 courtesy of The Metropolitan Museum of Art; number 25 by Geoffrey Clements.

Composition by A. Colish, Inc., Mount Vernon, N. Y.
Printed by The Meriden Gravure Company, Meriden, Conn.
Bound by A. Horowitz & Son, Clifton, N. J.